home
...Works

TURNING UP THE HEAT

REKINDLE ROMANCE *and* PASSION

BY TOMMY NELSON

SERENDIPITY
HOUSE

Turning Up the Heat: Rekindle Romance and Passion
© 2005 Tommy Nelson

Published by Serendipity House Publishers
Nashville, Tennessee

ISBN: 1-5749-4194-1

Dewey Decimal Classification: 306.8
Subject Headings: MARRIAGE \ INTIMACY \ DOMESTIC RELATIONS

Unless otherwise indicated, all Scripture quotations are taken from the *Holman Christian Standard Bible*®, Copyright © 1999, 2000, 2002, 2003 by Holman Bible Publishers. Used by permission.

Scriptures marked NASB taken from the *New American Standard Bible*®, © 1960, 1962, 1963, 1968, 1971, 1972, 1973, 1975, 1977, 1995 by the Lockman Foundation. Used by permission.

Scriptures marked NIV are taken from the *Holy Bible, New International Version,* Copyright © 1973, 1978, 1984 by International Bible Society. Used by permission.

To purchase additional copies of this resource or other studies:
ORDER ONLINE at www.SerendipityHouse.com;
WRITE Serendipity House, 117 10th Avenue North, Nashville, TN 37234
FAX (615) 277-8181   PHONE (800) 525-9563

SERENDIPITY®
H O U S E
1-800-525-9563
www.SerendipityHouse.com

Printed in the United States of America
11 10 09 08 07 06 05   1 2 3 4 5 6 7 8 9 10

CONTENTS

CROCODILES!

Once upon a time, an adventuresome world traveler visited a city in a distant land where he'd never been before. He was eager to observe local customs, so he went to a busy café on the banks of the river that wound through the heart of town and began to people-watch.

All of a sudden, the biggest crocodile our adventurer had ever seen lunged from the river, seized a man sitting at a table on the sidewalk in front of the café, and started dragging him toward the water. The traveler jumped to his feet. "Help! Help!" he shouted, "Somebody do something!"

Nobody else in the café reacted at all. People looked away from the man and the crocodile. They kept eating and just talked louder to be heard over the sounds of struggle. In desperation, the explorer ran to the river's edge and grabbed the man's arm as the crocodile started pulling him under. The man screamed in pain as the visitor yanked him free. The victim lost a portion of his leg, but an ambulance arrived in time to save his life.

The traveler returned to the café and called to the patrons, "Why didn't anybody do anything?" No one looked at him. No one answered. They went on as though he weren't there. "What is wrong with you people?" he shouted.

The owner of the café rushed to the angry visitor. "Please, please," he said soothingly, "Don't upset yourself so. You see, in our culture, it's embarrassing to talk about crocodiles or acknowledge they're around."

The traveler was startled by this custom. However, as he toured the city over the next several days, it was obvious that an unusual number of people were missing arms and legs. Many carried scars where big chunks had been torn out of their body. Additionally, he discovered from public records that nearly everybody had lost a family member to one of the river crocodiles. But nothing was less acceptable than to talk about crocodiles.

You hold in your hands a study guide about sex. Sex is a "crocodile." Every one of us can name one or more family members who have lost parts of themselves through misapplied sexuality. Some of you have been hurt deeply by your own run-in with this croc. We need to deal with it, but we don't talk about it in most of our churches. Consequently, the crocodiles just keep coming and chewing people up while others look away and clam up.

Meanwhile, Christians manage to take the book of the Bible that focuses on the truth about sexuality and treat it as symbolism concerning Christ and the church. We need to let God's Word speak loudly and clearly about sexuality. In marriage, the biggest problems are communication, sex, finances, and in-laws, in that order. When we don't communicate about sexuality, we combine and magnify the top two problems. As we do discuss sexuality in *Turning Up the Heat*, we are tackling the two biggest problems at the same time.

THE SONG OF SONGS

Wouldn't it be great if there were a book in the Bible that addressed pressing issues about love, sex, and marriage? Maybe young people wouldn't be so stressed about dating and single living. Maybe married couples could handle conflict, keep romance alive, and avoid divorce. Wouldn't it be great?

Well, there is! God put the Song of Songs in the Bible to meet those very needs, but most people act like it isn't there. When they find it, they squirm, struggle for composure, and conclude piously, "This must be an allegory about Christ and the church."

But it isn't just an allegory. King Solomon met a pretty, sunburned country girl who worked in one of his vineyards, and they fell in love. That almost sounds scandalous—a rich boss taking advantage of a poor but honest working girl. Nothing could be further from the truth. Two mature adults met one another eye-to-eye, heart-to-heart, and spirit-to-spirit. They weren't listed on the same page of the social register either.

Eventually, Solomon wrote this passionate love poem. It isn't easy to understand. It consists primarily of dialogue with little narration about setting, plot, and the passage of time. The speakers aren't identified, and it isn't always obvious when speakers change. The cast consists of Solomon, the girl, her brothers, a narrator, and a group identified as "the young women of Jerusalem," who have their say every now and then like the chorus out of an ancient Greek play.

We may find some of Solomon's imagery quaint, because we are separated from him by many years and cultural shifts. However, we will never find his passion quaint—or hers. Here's how the story goes:

- *First Meetings and Impressions (1:1—2:7)*
- *Their Courtship (2:8—3:5)*
- *Their Wedding (3:6-11)*
- *Their Honeymoon (4:1—5:1)*
- *Conflicts (5:2—6:3)*
- *Conflicts Resolved (6:4-13)*
- *Their Relationship Deepens (7:1—8:4)*
- *Renewed Commitment (8:5-14)*

Interspersed throughout *Turning Up the Heat*, we will look at several passages from different sections of the Song of Songs. As we do, it may be helpful to refer to this introduction to place an individual Scripture reference in the general context of the entire poem. We'll get a picture of the developed, mature love between Solomon and a country girl. Enjoy the poetry. Feel the power of this couple's love and commitment. You are sure to find some of God's truth that will change your marriage for the better in this unique part of God's instruction manual for life.

Generating "Heat"

INGREDIENTS: ROMANCE; PASSION; INTIMACY

God intended marriage to be romantic, passionate, and intimate. We read a statement like that and feel hopeful. Wouldn't it be great if that were true in more marriages? Well, why isn't it? The answer seems to be that too many of us are afraid to take the risk of talking with our spouses about sexuality.

Sexuality is as personal as a topic gets. In order to talk about our sexuality, we have to become vulnerable with each other at the deepest level of the most intimate area of our lives. We have to talk with our spouses about what only they have a right to know. But, frankly, a lot of us aren't sure we want to risk misunderstanding or rejection at such a personal level.

Most of us are studying *Turning Up the Heat: Rekindle Romance and Passion* because we've decided it's time to risk more than we have up until now. We're interested in seeing what God has to say about romance and passion. During the six sessions of this small-group study, we'll consider the importance of romance and intimacy in marriage, male and female perspectives on romance and intimacy, and practical ways to enhance these vital areas of a marriage relationship.

Breaking the Ice   10 - 15 MINUTES

LEADER: Be sure to read the introductory material (page 4) and the Leader's Guide (page 87) before the first session. Take a few minutes for group members to introduce themselves. "Breaking the Ice" questions are intended to get people talking to one another more than to approach the topic of the lesson. You may want to use all three questions in this first session to acquaint group members with one another.

1. How romantic would you say you are?

   ○ I'm about as romantic as a rock.
   ○ Feelings I have. Mush I can't muster.
   ○ I'm no movie star, but I can play a love scene.
   ○ I should be a romantic movie star!
   ○ Other: _____ .

2. We all had embarrassing moments in our early years of dating. Describe one you recall.

3. Where did you pick up most of your early "sex education"? Did it help you or hinder you in adjusting to married life?

   ○ Classes at school
   ○ Movies or television
   ○ Parents
   ○ Friends or neighbors
   ○ Church
   ○ Books or magazines
   ○ The locker room
   ○ Other: _____

Discovering the Truth
25-30 MINUTES

"Romance" is a word with a complicated family tree. Back in the Dark Ages, Latin was the language all educated Europeans spoke and wrote. No matter what the common people spoke in a given locale, the theologians and politicians did their work in Latin. Latin crossed all borders and united the elite at the top of all societies. All formal documents were written in Latin.

At the same time, Latin in distorted forms exerted tremendous influence on the everyday speech of the emerging kingdoms of Europe. Modern languages, such as Italian, French, and Spanish, are called Romance languages because of the impact of the "Roman" tongue on them. That sounds noble and sophisticated to modern ears, but a Romance language was actually the vulgar, corrupt speech of peasants and commoners.

Latin was for scholars, theologians, and diplomats. Latin was for solemn, lofty topics. A Romance language was for ordinary people and for common, earthy subjects. When the first poems and stories were written in vernacular languages instead of Latin, they were called "romances." Because so many "romances" were love stories, *romance* became a synonym for the relationship of a man and woman in love.

So romance has always involved words—everyday words by everyday people to describe the passions and delights of love. If we can feel love and speak words, we are all capable of romance. If we work at it, we are capable of great romance.

Romantic Words

As we read the poetry of Song of Songs 4:1-7, we see Solomon's romantic description of his bride. These are his words from his honeymoon night, and they get pretty steamy. The imagery sounds strange because it's from a distant time and place, but the passion shines through clearly. Solomon understood romance involves words and he didn't hesitate to use them. The message was, "You are wonderful to me."

> ¹ [Man:] *How beautiful you are, my darling. How very beautiful! Behind your veil, your eyes are doves. Your hair is like a flock of goats streaming down Mount Gilead.*
> ² *Your teeth are like a flock of newly shorn [sheep] coming up from washing, each one having a twin, and not one missing.* ³ *Your lips are like a scarlet cord, and your mouth is lovely. Behind your veil, your brow is like a slice of pomegranate.* ⁴ *Your neck is like the tower of David, constructed in layers. A thousand bucklers are hung on it— all of them shields of warriors.*
> ⁵ *Your breasts are like two fawns, twins of a gazelle, that feed among the lilies.*
> ⁶ *Before the day breaks and the shadows flee, I will make my way to the mountain of myrrh and the hill of frankincense.*⁷ *You are absolutely beautiful, my darling, with no imperfection in you.*
>
> SONG OF SONGS 4:1-7

1. What might motivate a new husband, such as Solomon, to praise the beauty of his bride? To what aspects of his bride does he focus his praise?

2. How do you think Solomon's beloved felt when her new husband so openly appreciated her, detailing the features of her beauty? How might genuine, tender words have affected her willingness to give herself to her husband?

3. This young wife worked hard in the fields, so how could Solomon say she "had no imperfection" (verse 7)? How can those of us who are less than perfect physical specimens genuinely praise each other's appearance?

4. Why is romance with tender words and tender touch so important to women in particular?

5. With the passage of time, what are some reasons many married couples become less vocal about their physical delight in one another? What does that do to the level of romance in their relationship and lovemaking?

Although every couple is unique, men are generally more interested in sex while women are more interested in romance. Author and speaker Gary Smalley says men are microwaves and women are Crock-Pots™. A man's wife walks into the bedroom. Bing. He's ready. Maybe they haven't spoken all evening. Maybe they fought all evening. It doesn't matter. That's the way a man is wired. A woman, however, is a Crock-Pot™. She isn't stimulated as quickly or as much visually; she's aroused slowly by a tender, appreciative man who doesn't take her for granted. That's the way a woman is wired.

Marriage starts with romance. To be romantic, a husband has to say, "I love you." He has to be able to tell his wife that she's wonderful, in whatever ways she is wonderful. It has been said that a woman's greatest sex organ is her mind, so tender words and tender touches are important. On the other side of that coin, if a man is abusive, angry, unkind, or immoral, his wife will not think highly of him. She will have no inclination to give herself to him sexually.

Capturing the Heart

After Solomon described and praised the beauty of his bride, he invited his bride to come into the safety of his arms and away from the frightening world about her. His bride had captured his heart, and he had willingly yielded it to her. Romance depends on our willingness to keep surrendering our hearts to each other.

> [8] [Man:] Come with me from Lebanon, my bride—with me from Lebanon! Descend from the peak of Amana, from the summit of Senir and Hermon, from the dens of the lions, from the mountains of the leopards.
> [9] You have captured my heart, my sister, my bride. You have captured my heart with one glance of your eyes, with one jewel of your necklace.

10 How delightful your love is, my sister, my bride. Your love is much better than wine, and the fragrance of your perfume than any balsam.
11 Your lips drip [sweetness like] the honeycomb, my bride. Honey and milk are under your tongue. The fragrance of your garments is like the fragrance of Lebanon.

SONG OF SONGS 4:8-11

6. Where would you say is a good place for newlyweds to celebrate their honeymoon? What places have been sites of romantic retreats for you? What made them good places to enjoy one another?

7. What role do you think clothing, grooming, and scent play (verses 9-11) in creating romantic encounters for married couples? How much time and effort would it take to employ these to capture your spouse's heart?

8. Verse 9 says, "You have captured my heart." What are some ways husbands and wives can continue to capture the hearts of their marriage partners?

Men tend to be very romantic while courting. They send flowers every day for six months. They take their sweethearts out every weekend and lavish attention on them. After they marry these same women, the flowers often dry up, the dates disappear, and the attention turns to football, NASCAR, a career, or just the business of life. In the same way that romance is vital in bringing love to life during courtship, romance remains vital in marriage for fanning the flames to keep love alive and strong.

Husband, continue to capture your wife's heart. Keep courting her. Make dates with her and show her attention. Plan ahead and take the initiative to set everything up. Clean up. Be spontaneous. Buy her little gifts for no reason than your love for her. Don't forget words are part of romance.

Wife, keep capturing the heart of your husband by being responsive to him. Show him appreciation for what he does for your family. Express gratitude for projects he does around the house. When he gives his heart to you in romance, be sure he knows your heart is his.

These ongoing little actions can energize your marriage.

A NOTE: Perhaps you fear responding to your husband because he misinterprets the slightest response as an invitation to have sex. You may have to tell him that and try to arrive at an understanding about how to communicate clearly so you can enjoy tender words and tender touches for their own sake too.

Embracing the Truth
10-15 MINUTES

LEADER: This section focuses on helping couples begin to integrate what they have learned from the Bible into their own marriages ... where the "rubber meets the road."

Rekindling Desire

In this final scene of the honeymoon, Solomon refers to the sexuality of his bride by means of images of a garden of fruit and spices, a spring, and a well. The garden metaphor occurs frequently in the Song of Songs. In verse 16, Solomon's bride responds to him and offers herself to him.

> ¹² [Man:] *My sister, my bride, [you are] a locked garden—a locked garden and a sealed spring.*
> ¹³ *Your branches are a paradise of pomegranates with choicest fruits, henna with nard—*¹⁴ *nard and saffron, calamus and cinnamon, with all the trees of frankincense, myrrh and aloes, with all the best spices.*
> ¹⁵ *[You are] a garden spring, a well of flowing water streaming from Lebanon.* ¹⁶ *[Woman:] Awaken, north wind—come, south wind. Blow on my garden, and spread the fragrance of its spices. Let my love come to his garden and eat its choicest fruits.*
> SONG OF SONGS 4:12-16

1. How is verse 12 a picture of wife's virginity before marriage? What happens with the "locked garden" and "sealed spring" in marriage?

2. How could Solomon's bride have been so forthright in giving herself to him? From his words, how did it seem like he would treat her in his passion? How confident must she have been in how he would treat her sexually?

3. It's easy to believe a newly married couple had a strong desire for one another sexually, but we can still learn from their dialogue. How can we keep alive the emotional and physical desire for one another over the long haul in marriage? What roles do communication and consideration play?

In the fourth chapter of the Song of Songs, we've seen Solomon talk to his bride and undress her. Her hair is down, her veil is off, and he has removed her dress. He has looked at the bareness of her body and praised her.

In verse 5 of this intimate passage, Solomon compared his bride's breasts to "two fawns, twins of a gazelle, that feed among the lilies." Implicit in that comparison is gentleness, because that's how deer should be approached. If the first quality of marital love is romance, the second is gentleness. Movies and television may portray sexual activity as though it was an Olympic sport, but usually it is best when tenderness and consideration lead the way.

Solomon and his bride were on their honeymoon, so it's easy to believe they had a strong desire for one another sexually. Maintaining that kind of mutual desire for one another through the life of a marriage depends on both partners committing themselves to giving pleasure to the other. From the husband's side, a lot of this depends on gentleness and patient attentiveness to what pleases his wife. From the wife's side, a lot of this depends on her responsiveness to what is pleasurable in her husband's lovemaking.

♥ Connecting

15 MINUTES

LEADER: Use "Connecting" as a time to begin to bond with, encourage, and support one another. Invite everyone to join in and to be open with one another, but allow members who don't wish to share on a particular topic to pass.

The "Connecting" segment of each small-group session provides an opportunity for group members to tell one another their life stories. As you learn one another's stories in greater detail, your relationships will mature and deepen. Enjoy these encounters and the friendships they nurture.

1. We all enter marriage with wrong expectations. When you got married, what were some of your misconceptions about how sex would work and the role it would play in marriage?

2. What physical characteristics of your spouse attracted you when you began dating?

3. What kinds of verbal expressions by your husband or wife make you feel good and strengthen your closeness as a couple?

LEADER: Take some extra time in this first session to go over the Group Covenant on page 94 at the back of this book. Now would be a great time for everyone to pass around their books to collect contact information in the Group Directory on page 104 (last page) of each book.

Record group prayer requests, and pray regularly for them between now and the next session. In addition to these requests, pray together now for each couple that they will come to know greater romance, passion, and intimacy through the course of the *Turning Up the Heat* study.

Prayer Requests:

🏠 Taking It Home

You do not have to share anything from this "Taking It Home" session with your small group, although you will have opportunity to do so. Take some time in the next few days to reflect alone, and with your spouse, about this first session of *Turning Up the Heat*.

(1) Questions to Take to Your Heart on page 17

(2) A Date Night on page 18

When? _____ Where? _____

SNEAK PEEK

Next time we meet, we'll consider some of the foundational characteristics that make sexuality within marriage a joyous and sacred mystery.

QUESTIONS TO TAKE TO YOUR HEART

You've read the first section of *Turning Up the Heat*, and participated in the discussion with your small group. As you approach this question to take to your heart, don't analyze it intellectually; rather, look into your heart to find where your true attitudes and unexamined motives lurk. Grapple with what drives your thinking and behavior. Dig for what you really believe in the deep recesses of your heart about God, yourself, your spouse, and the world in which you live. Be sure to record your thoughts, feelings, and fresh insights.

✢ Am I working to capture the heart of my spouse with the same energy and passion I did before we were married or in the early years of our marriage?

✢ What's hindering me from pursuing deeper romance, passion, and intimacy? What false belief or pattern of self-protection might I have accepted?

DATE NIGHT

Before the next *Turning Up the Heat* session, make a date to have dinner at your favorite restaurant. It needs to be quiet and private enough so you can talk freely and comfortably. Each of you should take a favorite childhood photograph of the other as the basis for your after-dinner conversation. Tell one another what you can see of the adult in the picture of the child. For instance, the twinkle in the child's eyes foreshadows the adult's love of fun, or the set of the child's mouth and chin suggests the determination the adult still has. (Think about this in advance so you aren't trying to figure out what to say while you're trying to listen to your spouse.)

When you are talking, you will be expressing your insight into and your appreciation of your mate. When you are listening, you will be receiving your mate's insight into and appreciation of you. Listening and receiving are very important to this date. Accept and value everything your spouse says about you.

When you arrive home from your dinner date, place the childhood photographs side by side in your bedroom or family room—somewhere you both will see them frequently in days to come. Tell one another, "I love the woman this girl became" or "I love the man this boy became." Hold hands and pray together thanking God for the gift of your spouse and for what he or she brings into your life and relationship.

SCRIPTURE NOTES

SONG OF SONGS 4:1-16

4:1 Behind your veil, your eyes. A veil may have covered the beloved's face, but the lover still saw the beauty underneath, as well as in her eyes. *a flock of goats streaming down.* Goats common in Canaan were generally black; the lover saw his beloved's dark hair cascading down. It may have been loosened to fall free from an elaborate wedding hairstyle.

4:2 newly shorn [sheep]. The sheep would thus have been clean and white.

4:3 Your lips ... scarlet. Egyptian women often painted their lips, and her beautiful lips incite the lover's desire to kiss her.

4:4 Your neck is like the tower. Her neck, adorned with beautiful necklaces, was long, strong, and straight as a military tower.

4:5 two fawns. Fawns are young, sweet, delicate, and soft (8:8).

4:6 Before the day breaks. Their wedding night would be long and passionate. *mountain of myrrh ... hill of frankincense.* Another reference to the beloved's breasts.

4:9 captured my heart, my sister. As Solomon's wife, she was now part of his royal family. In love poetry of the ancient Near East, lovers often call each other "brother" and "sister" (vv. 10,12; 5:1) as terms of endearment.

4:11 Your lips drip [sweetness like] the honeycomb. Her words of love were rich and sweet to him (Prov. 16:24). Love's delights were often described with images of sweetness in the ancient Near East. See also Proverbs 5:3 and 16:24.

4:12 garden. A garden is full of beauty, refreshment, and sensual delight—a beautiful description of love (v. 16; 5:1; 6:2). *Locked ... locked ... sealed.* References to the beloved's virginity before the wedding night or perhaps even her exclusive relationship with her lover.

4:14-15 all the best spices. The perfumed aromas were sensual and rich, and many of these spices were used in the temple anointing oil. The beloved desires the winds to blow her charming fragrances to her lover, drawing him to her.

4:16 Awaken. Both previous references to sexuality had insisted that love not be awakened before the wedding (2:7; 3:5). *Let my love come to his garden.* The beloved bride invited her lover to enjoy her sexual pleasures for the first time. He expressed his complete satisfaction as a result in 5:1.

Striking the Match

BIRDS ... BEES ... IT'S ALL GOOD

In the first session of *Turning Up the Heat*, we discussed romance and intimacy. We looked at the importance of tender words and tender touch. We considered the necessity of continuing to captivate, and be captivated by, our spouses. Finally, we explored ways to rekindle desire and longing for each other sexually. While there's much more to romance than sexual activity, sexual contact is the final stage of romance between a husband and wife.

In this second session, we'll consider some foundational biblical principles about sexuality in marriage. Deeply satisfying sexual relations begin with a good grasp of how God has made us and understanding what He intended for His gift of sexuality.

Breaking the Ice   10 - 15 MINUTES

LEADER: The "Breaking the Ice" questions will help group members get better acquainted and begin talking casually about the session topic. Keep the tone of the conversation light and be sure everyone gets a turn. You may use any or all of this icebreakers that fit your group.

1. Which section of the newspaper best describes your family's communication about sex when you were growing up?

   ○ One-liner hidden in the obituaries – I was never quite sure my parents even knew about sex.

   ○ Short article in local news section – We had the "talk" and nothing was ever to be said again.

   ○ Front Page feature story – We had the "talk" with great fanfare and enthusiasm.

   ○ Scattered through the life section – It was definitely not a subject for dinner discussion, but I got the gist!

   ○ Headliner in every section – You name it, we discussed it!

2. Which movie title best describes what you learned about sex from your church or other religious sources as you were growing up?

○ *The Bodyguard* – We can't control sexual urges so be sure to use protection.

○ *The Seven Year Itch* – Except for the rare occurrences for having children, sex is sinful.

○ *The Invisible Man* – Sex has nothing to do with your walk with God.

○ *As Good As It Gets* – Sex is a gift from God for the married couples.

○ *The Fast and the Furious* – Grab all the pleasure you can.

○ Other: _____ .

3. When you were growing up, did you expect to get married or did you expect to remain single? What influences shaped your thinking? What were you looking forward to in marriage?

LEADER: Encourage each person to share a key insight from "A Question to Take to Your Heart" or "Date Night." This should only take a couple of minutes each, but allow a little more time if someone has something inspiring to share. Affirm couples who connected especially well.

4. How did your "Taking It Home" activities go? Would you like to share a key insight from your date night or from the question to your heart about capturing the heart of your mate?

Discovering the Truth

25-30 MINUTES

LEADER: In each section of "Discovering the Truth," ask various group members to read the Bible passages. Be sure to leave at least 15 minutes for the "Connecting" segment later in your session.

Most of us probably entered marriage woefully ignorant of sexuality. We may have known the biology of reproduction from school. We may have seen enough television programs and movies to think we knew everything about sexual intimacy. But we didn't know nearly as much as we thought we did.

Most of us entered marriage with a vague notion that sexual activity was somehow a little dirty. It had been off limits. Maybe we had heard sermons against premarital and extramarital sex. Maybe we had seen family members and friends scarred by bad sexual experiences. So, we got married and didn't know whether or not it was quite proper to talk in the daylight about what we did in the dark.

God created and gives guidance about our sexuality. If we listen to Him, we can talk to one another openly from the same biblical perspective.

God Said, "Sex Is Good!"

The creation account in Genesis reports Adam delight and excitement about Eve when he first saw her. The teaching from the Bible supports the position that sex is from God and it is good.

> [23] And the man said: This one, at last, is bone of my bone, and flesh of my flesh; this one will be called woman, for she was taken from man.
> [24] This is why a man leaves his father and mother and bonds with his wife, and they become one flesh. [25] Both the man and his wife were naked, yet felt no shame.
>
> GENESIS 2:23-25

> [18] Let your fountain be blessed, and take pleasure in the wife of your youth.
> [19] A loving doe, a graceful fawn – let her breasts always satisfy you; be lost in her love forever.
>
> PROVERBS 5:18-19

> Enjoy life with the wife you love all the days of your fleeting life, which has been given to you under the sun, all your fleeting days. For that is your portion in life and in your struggle under the sun.
>
> ECCLESIASTES 9:9

LEADER: Discuss as many discovery questions as time permits. The strongest application questions appear in the "Embracing the Truth" section, but this section also has some application questions. It will help to highlight in advance the questions you don't want to miss.

1. Why was Adam delighted with Eve (Genesis 2:23)? What do verses 24-25 conclude from Adam's excitement about marriage?

2. Why do you think God wants a husband and wife to find completion and pleasure in one another? What do Genesis 2, Proverbs 5, and Ecclesiastes 9 highlight as some reasons God created sex?

3. Why do you suppose God chose sexual union to picture the complementary unity of husband and wife (verse 24)?

4. What do you think it is about marriage that makes it possible to take delight in and be "lost" in the love of one person for life (Proverbs 5:18-19 and Ecclesiastes 9:9)?

5. How do the oneness and pleasure provided by marriage help a couple survive the struggles of life "under the sun" (Ecclesiastes 9:9)?

For centuries the church taught that original sin was tied up with sex in some way and sex was morally suspect. Nothing could be further from the truth. God designed and blessed human sexuality. All animals copulate, but only humans make love. While human sexual activity is the means for reproducing the species, it plays a central role in creating and expressing intimacy between husbands and wives. God had sexual pleasure, intimacy, and romance in mind when He designed our sexual dimension.

Sexuality is the fireplace of our marriages. The fireplace generates heat and light. It creates an atmosphere of cozy warmth. It's the center of a contented family. Marriage is not just a working partnership between a guy who's a mechanic and a woman who cooks, cares for kids, and cleans windows. A marriage is rooted in passion. That's what we were thinking when we went into it. That's the way God wants it to be too..

God Said, "Sex Is Sacred!"

The Old Testament and New Testament uniformly limit sexual contact to the confines of marriage. Within marriage, the Bible commends lovemaking as right and delightful. God is clearly interested that married couples express their sexuality in ways that benefit their union and enhance their lives. He warns us about dangerous sexual activities.

[15] Drink water from your own cistern, water flowing from your own well.
[16] Should your springs flow in the streets, streams of water in the public squares?
[17] They should be for you alone and not for you [to share] with strangers.

PROVERBS 5:15-17

[18] Flee from sexual immorality! "Every sin a person can commit is outside the body," but the person who is sexually immoral sins against his own body. [19] Do you not know that your body is a sanctuary of the Holy Spirit who is in you, whom you have from God? You are not your own, [20] for you were bought at a price; therefore glorify God in your body.

I CORINTHIANS 6:18-20

[2] But because of sexual immorality, each man should have his own wife, and each woman should have her own husband. [3] A husband should fulfill his marital duty to his wife, and likewise a wife to her husband. ... [5] Do not deprive one another — except when you agree, for a time, to devote yourselves to prayer. Then come together again; otherwise, Satan may tempt you because of your lack of self-control.

I CORINTHIANS 7:2-3,5

[4] Marriage must be respected by all, and the marriage bed kept undefiled, because God will judge immoral people and adulterers.

HEBREWS 13:4

6. Why does God put limits on sexuality? What reasons does He give for refraining from immorality (Proverbs 5:15-17; I Corinthians 6:18-20)?

7. Which of these do you think best explains the idea of "marital duty" in I Corinthians 7:2-3,5?

   ○ Husbands and wives should have sex with their spouse whenever requested.
   ○ Husbands and wives should always consider their spouse's desires when making sexual decisions.
   ○ Husbands and wives should never make selfish sexual demands.
   ○ Husbands and wives should be careful about refusing their spouse's sexual advances.
   ○ Other: _____ .

8. From what you know of the Bible, what kinds of sexual practices and attitudes would God see as defiling or damaging marriage (Hebrews 13:4)?

God's boundaries restrict us from following harmful paths and redirect us toward positive behaviors. We're never happier or more content in life than when we live freely inside the limits of His law and love. Nowhere is this truer than in our sexuality.

The Ten Commandments forbid adultery (Exodus 20:14), and the New Testament repeatedly condemns premarital and extramarital sexual activity. The biblical standard always is "a man leaves his father and mother and bonds with his wife" (Genesis 2:24). Sexual activity and attention within marriage have tremendous positive potential; sexual activity and attention outside of marriage have tremendous negative potential.

Marital sexuality also carries responsibilities. Lovemaking doesn't occur in marriage just because a man and woman are excited. Sometimes it's an act of service on the part of one spouse. In essence that person says, "You have a need and I'll meet it." At that point, sex becomes an act of selfless love.

Embracing the Truth
10-15 MINUTES

LEADER: This section focuses on helping couples begin to integrate what they have learned from the Bible into their own marriages As they continue to grasp more of God's plan for their intimacy.

God Said, "Sex Requires Understanding"

What the Bible says to husbands and wives about married life assumes they know one another very well. Perhaps we miss that because it's so obvious. Biblical teaching about respect, leadership, and love cannot be implemented successfully when marriage partners don't understand one another and don't communicate well. If we reflect on successful and unsuccessful marriages we have observed, we'll realize that is true.

> *Acquire wisdom—how much better it is than gold! And acquire understanding—it is preferable to silver.*
>
> PROVERBS 16:16

> [1] *Wives, in the same way, submit yourselves to your own husbands so that, even if some disobey the [Christian] message, they may be won over without a message by the way their wives live,* [2] *when they observe your pure, reverent lives. ...* [7] *Husbands, in the same way, live with your wives with understanding of their weaker nature yet showing them honor as co-heirs of the grace of life, so that your prayers will not be hindered.*
>
> 1 PETER 3:1-2,7

1. What did Peter infer or expect wives to understand about their husbands (1 Peter 3:1-2)? How do you think a wife can gain those insights into her husband's mind and heart that are more precious than gold?

2. What did Peter expect husbands to understand about their wives (verse 7)? How do you think husbands can gain those insights more precious than gold? What does "weaker nature" refer to?

3. Which of these hindrances to understanding your spouse do you think would be most damaging to a marriage? Why?

○ Feelings of disdain for your spouse
○ Attentiveness to other men or women
○ Feelings of insecurity and defensiveness
○ Pride and selfishness
○ An attitude of critical perfectionism or lack of honor
○ Preoccupation with work or children
○ Other: _____

4. What have you found to be the best opportunities for gaining insight into your spouse?

Good sexual behavior is a learned skill. It's amazing how many married people think they're just supposed to know automatically how to please one other. In an ideal world, parents would train their children in matters of sexuality. In an ideal church, older men would mentor younger men about marital sexuality, and older women would mentor younger women.

Husbands and wives should be lifelong learners concerning their mates. A husband is to live with his wife "with understanding" (1 Peter 3:7). A wife is to be aware of her husband's spiritual condition and be careful how her lifestyle influences that condition (verses 1-4). Remember, sexuality is the fireplace of the marriage. When the fireplace isn't working properly, the whole marriage takes on a chilly atmosphere. Fortunately, it's never too late to rekindle the fire.

♡ Connecting 15 MINUTES

We have an opportunity in this "Connecting" activity to become better acquainted while sharing our thoughts about intimacy in marriage. It's only the second session in *Turning Up the Heat*, so we won't get too personal. We don't need too much heat this quickly! We'll focus on the collective wisdom in the group about intimacy and knowing our partners.

1. Which statement best describes what you thought when you were first married about sex being good or dirty? Has your perspective changed?

   ○ Sex is for procreation, not pleasure.
   ○ Sex is sinful, because the great fall in the Garden of Eden involved sex.
   ○ Sex is something to endure for the sake of my marriage.
   ○ Sex was forbidden in my life for so long, it has to be a little bad.
   ○ Sex is going to be the best thing ever.
   ○ Sex is good because God made it.
   ○ Other: _____.

2. What things have you learned about your spouse that you most admire and respect? How did you discover these things?

3. Which of the following truths do you find to be the greatest struggle for you? Please explain.

   ○ Sex is good – We are supposed to enjoy each other.
   ○ Sex is sacred – There are necessary boundaries.
   ○ Sex requires understanding – It's not automatic.
   ○ Other: _____.

Record group prayer requests, and pray regularly for them. Give thanks through the week for the positive qualities that your mate possesses. Pray now that each person will embrace the truth of sex the way God intended it.

Prayer Requests:

🏠 Taking It Home

LEADER: "Taking It Home" from Session One featured "Questions to Take to Your Heart." This time there's "A Question to Take to God." Again, there's a couple's activity to reinforce the session content and help couples strengthen their marriages. Keep encouraging everyone to complete both projects before the next session.

You are the source of your mate's sexual delight and pleasure, and your mate is yours. Use "A Question to Take to God" to discover God's intentions for romance and intimacy in your marriage. The "Date Night" activity gives you a chance to have fun together and hopefully increase your understanding of one another. Set aside enough time to give your full attention to these activities.

(1) A Question to Take to God on page 30

(2) A Date Night on page 31

LEADER: Have each couple set a date, time, and location for the "Date Night" ... right now before you close your session.

When? _____ Where? _____

SNEAK PEEK
Next time we meet, we will consider some of the differences between male and female sexuality that make "turning up the heat" a challenge.

A Question to Take to God

Studying and discussing God's truth is not an end in itself. The goal is heart and life change. To take the next step of integrating the truth into our lives, we need to (1) look honestly into our hearts to understand the innermost motivations that drive us and (2) seek God's perspective on where we are, where we should be, and the path we should take. When you ask God a question, expect His Spirit to guide your heart into truth. Don't manufacture an answer. Just pose the question to God and wait on Him. (Remember: the litmus test for anything we hear from God is alignment with the Bible as our ultimate truth source). Be sure to keep a journal of the insights you gain from your times with God.

✦ God, help me see Your desire for the romantic and sexual dimensions of our marriage. Are there attitudes and perspectives on romance or sex that I need to change?

DATE NIGHT

Before the third *Turning Up the Heat* session, go see a movie together just for fun. Try to find one you'd both like to see.

After the show, take home some ice cream and toppings to make sundaes. Over dessert, discuss two questions that will deepen your insight into your sexual relationship with your mate. The first question is historical and the second is informational:

(1) What do you remember about our sexual encounters early on in our marriage? What made these special?

(2) What has been for you the most pleasurable sexual encounter we've had? The answer to that question may reinforce what you already know or give you new insights to process. Do not question or downplay your lover's responses. Take very seriously what you hear, and think about it in the days to come.

Thank one another for sharing intensely private reactions to your lovemaking. Hold hands or embrace as you pray together, asking God to deepen your relationship with each other.

Scripture Notes

GENESIS 2:23-25

2:23 woman ... taken from man. In Hebrew, "man" is *ish*; "woman" is ishah. Ishah is not derived from *ish*, but it sounds like it. Biblical Hebrew was a poetic language. Its speakers and writers loved word plays, so it is said that *Ishah* was taken out of *ish*. Adam and Eve understood the implications of that.

2:24 leaves ... and bonds. From the beginning of creation, God established the order of the family. Just as Eve was made from Adam's own body, so when a couple is married, the two become one. A man leaves his home, the roots from which he came, and establishes a new life with his new family. Even though polygamy was practiced in the Old Testament times, it is clear from this verse that God's plan was for a man and a woman to become one in lifelong service and union.

2:25 naked ... no shame. Before the fall of paradise, Adam and Eve felt no need to conceal anything. They had never disappointed or hurt one another. It never crossed their minds to criticize, accuse, or blame the other or to fear receiving criticism, accusation, or blame.

PROVERBS 5:15-19

5:15 own cistern ... own well. Imagery referring to a man's own wife.

5:16 in the streets ... public squares. Imagery referring to promiscuous behavior.

5:18 fountain. Euphemism for the male sexual organ.

5:19 doe ... fawn. The animal imagery depicts the young wife as graceful and, perhaps, shy.

ECCLESIASTES 9:9

9:9 fleeting life ... fleeting days. Much of the Book of Ecclesiastes forces readers to consider the futility of life that is lived without relation to God. It is frighteningly brief. *under the sun.* Life apart from God is limited to what you see here below on earth. One of the few bright spots in this bleak picture is marital love.

1 CORINTHIANS 6:18-20

6:18 Flee. The temptation to sexual sin was so overwhelming in Corinth that Paul used this strong verb by way of command. The sexual impulse is so powerful that staying around temptation to fight it is foolish. Escaping is the wise option. *sins against his own body.* Adultery and other sexual sins use the body for base purposes when God intends it to be used for exalted purposes. Sexual sins disgrace the body.

6:19 You are not your own. Paul argued that our bodies belong to God because Christ bought us on the cross and because the Holy Spirit lives in our bodies in the same way God lived in the Old Testament tabernacle and temple.

1 CORINTHIANS 7:2-5

7:2 First, Paul said it is not good for a husband and wife to abstain from sexual relationship—since this would increase the temptation to commit adultery.

7:3 marital duty ... a wife to her husband. While it's true that in the experience of many married couples the man wants sexual relations more often than the woman, that isn't always the case. Husbands need to understand the sexual desires of their wives and respect them. However, mutual delight is an important goal for couples to discuss and pursue rather than pursuing sexual activity primarily to satisfy self.

7:5 deprive. Literally, "rob." For one partner to opt out of sexual relations under the guise of spirituality is a form of robbery. However, this verse is not a "club" to use on a disinterested mate. It's a warning about the spiritual dangers of sexual dysfunction. It is also a challenge for women to learn how to respond to their husbands, and for men to learn how to show tender physical affection to their wives. Abstinence is allowed under two conditions: both partners agree, and it is for a limited time. *prayer.* The purpose of such abstinence is prayer. *lack of self-control.* Paul assumes that a couple would not be married in the first place if they did not feel any sexual desire, and thus they ought to fulfill such desires legitimately, lest they be tempted to fall into adultery.

HEBREWS 13:4

13:4 Marriage. The denial of legitimate sexual desire led to incidents of sexual immorality (1 Corinthians 6:15-20). Here, marriage is validated, and people are warned not to be involved in any form of immorality (12:16).

1 PETER 3:1-2,7

3:1 in the same way. By this phrase, Peter made a transition from slaves to wives. Just as the behavior of Christ was the model for slaves, so too it was for women. *submit yourselves.* "Submit" translates the Greek word *hupotasso*. *Hupotasso* is compounded from *hupo*, the preposition meaning "under," and *tithemi*, the common Greek verb "to place." *Hupotasso* denoted that a woman voluntarily placed herself under her husband's leadership. *won over.* Peter (like Paul) did not counsel Christian women to leave unbelieving husbands. His desire was that the husbands eventually be converted.

3:7 Peter reminded husbands that the respect they are to show to all people (2:17) is also due their own wives. *in the same way.* Peter harkened back to the example of Christ who voluntarily gave Himself for the sake of others (2:21). *their weaker nature.* Literally, the "weaker vessel." There has been much debate about the meaning. It might refer to anatomical differences from men (this phrase was used in Greek to refer to the woman's body), to the inferior position of women in that society, to the comparative lack of physical strength in woman, or to women as having a more precious or fragile nature like fine china. While all these are true, the key message is that women accept a more vulnerable position when they submit to their husbands. *showing them honor.* Literally "assigning honor." This statement is an intentional paradox. In the Greco-Roman culture, women were treated as an inferior class and inferiors honored their superiors. Christ in stark contrast taught leaders to serve those they led (Matthew 20:25-26). *co-heirs.* Both husbands and wives are equal participants in the grace of God, again reinforcing the idea that men and women have equal value in God's eyes.

A Combustible Mixture

THE MYSTERY OF MEN; THE WONDER OF WOMEN

During our second session, we looked at some fundamental principles for enjoying a satisfying sexual relationship. God created sexuality as part of our humanity and pronounced it good along with other aspects of personality. God values human sexuality properly expressed. He praises the joys of marriage and carefully guards against distortions of His design for the expression of sexuality. He urges us to know our marriage partner and respond to him or her sensitively and lovingly.

During this session, we will turn our attention to differences between male and female sexuality and the implications of those differences for how we relate to one another as husband and wife.

Breaking the Ice   10 - 15 MINUTES

LEADER: The "Breaking the Ice" questions will relax people and help them continue to connect better with one another. You aren't looking for "right" answers, but rather for viewpoints group members hold and experiences they have had. Choose one or more icebreakers.

1. Which movie star or other popular entertainer best represents your ideal man? Your ideal woman?

2. When you were a child, what did you conclude about men from observing your dad and about women from observing your mom?

3. What were your favorite childhood toys that fit gender stereotypes? What toys did you like playing with that are associated with the other gender?

4. How did your "Taking It Home" activities go? Did you hear from God? Without going into particulars, how beneficial was the conversation you had on "Date Night"?

Discovering the Truth
20-25 MINUTES

The Microwave and the Crock Pot™

Gary Smalley was probably the first to say that when it comes to sexuality, men are microwaves and women are Crock Pots™.

1. In what ways would men in general be sexual microwaves? What does it mean that women are Crock Pots™? How can these differences create misunderstandings and hurt feelings?

The Apostle Paul wrote unique and nearly identical instructions for wives and husbands in letters to the Ephesians and to the Colossians. In both letters, Paul urged wives to be submissive (and respectful) to their husbands and husbands to love their wives. Because of the importance of how we relate to each other, God thought both wives and husbands needed to hear these commands twice. Let's read the more compact version from Colossians.

> [18] *Wives, submit to your husbands, as is fitting in the Lord.*
> [19] *Husbands, love your wives and do not be harsh with them.*
>
> COLOSSIANS 3:18-19 (NIV)

LEADER: Discuss as many discovery questions as time permits. The strongest application questions appear in "Embracing the Truth" section. It will help to highlight in advance the questions you don't want to miss.

Be familiar with the Scripture Notes at the end of this session to help clarify any issues. There are additional tips and helps in the Leader's Notes that begin on page 95.

2. What is there about the way many husbands tend to lead that makes it hard for wives to follow their lead? How would this apply in the sexual realm?

3. What have you observed about the way men and women relate to each other that can make it hard for many husbands to express love effectively?

4. Bitterness and harshness can be a problem for both husbands and wives. Why do you think husbands, rather than wives, are specifically warned against this (verse 19)?

5. God created men and women to be different (What on earth was He thinking?). How can we understand and capitalize on these differences?

We tend to expect our spouses to approach sexual relations the same way we do but that's not how we're wired. Stimulate a man visually and ding he's aroused. Sexual arousal for a woman, on the other hand, is a complex process that happens over time. She responds to attention, kindness, and admiration in the context of whole relationship. It mustn't be rushed into or away from.

Our differences require that we be lifelong students of each other, so we can understand these differences and use our insights to please one another emotionally and sexually. If we overcome our inhibitions and learn to talk (even during lovemaking) about our sexual contacts, we'll experience greater intimacy by risking such vulnerability.

Signals and Combinations

Samson and Delilah hardly stand out as sterling examples of anything good. However, they do exemplify interesting truths about reading the verbal and nonverbal signals men and women send one another in passionate situations. Delilah felt she knew how to get what she wanted. Samson thought he could get away with anything by repeating a winning formula. Samson and Delilah may have been using each other, but in that process, they were trying hard to read one another's signals.

LEADER: If time is short, summarize this story. Skip questions 6 and 7.

> [4] *Some time later, he [Samson] fell in love with a woman named Delilah, who lived in the Sorek Valley. [5] The Philistine leaders went to her and said, "Persuade him to tell you where his great strength comes from, so we can overpower him, tie him up, and make him helpless. Each of us will then give you 1,100 pieces of silver."*
> [6] *So Delilah said to Samson, "Please tell me, where does your great strength [come from]? How could [someone] tie you up and make you helpless?"*
> [7] *Samson told her, "If they tie me up with seven fresh bowstrings that have not been dried, I will become weak and be like any other man." ... [a lie that didn't work]*
> [10] *Then Delilah said to Samson, "You have mocked me and told me lies! Won't you please tell me how you can be tied up?" ... [When Delilah pleaded twice more, Samson told her 2 other lies that did not give the Philistines success either.]*

¹⁵ *"How can you say, 'I love you,'"* she told him, *"when your heart is not with me? This is the third time you have mocked me and not told me what makes your strength so great!"*

¹⁶ *Because she nagged him day after day and pled with him until she wore him out,* ¹⁷ *he told her the whole truth and said to her, "My hair has never been cut, because I am a Nazirite to God from birth. If I am shaved, my strength will leave me, and I will become weak and be like any other man."*

¹⁸ *When Delilah realized that he had told her the whole truth, she sent this message to the Philistine leaders: "Come one more time, for he has told me the whole truth." The Philistine leaders came to her and brought the money with them.*

¹⁹ *Then she let him fall asleep on her lap and called a man to shave off the seven braids on his head. In this way, she rendered him helpless, and his strength left him.* ²⁰ *Then she cried, "Samson, the Philistines are here!" When he awoke from his sleep, he said, "I will escape as I did before and shake myself free." But he did not know that the Lord had left him.*

JUDGES 16:4-7, 10,15-20

6. Why do you suppose Delilah felt confident that if she was determined in pleading with Samson he would give away the secret of his strength (Judges 16:6,10,15-17)?

7. Which of these sounds like the best explanation for why Samson told Delilah the truth about his strength (verse 17)?

   ○ He preferred death to further nagging.
   ○ She so sexually aroused him that he lost control and told the truth.
   ○ He was overconfident about his strength and felt invincible.
   ○ He never thought anyone could shave his head without waking him, even after sex.
   ○ Other: _____ .

8. How is knowing your spouse's "signals" about his or her sexual availability constructive to relational harmony? How might that knowledge be used manipulatively?

9. What was the formula Samson kept using to keep Delilah off track. Why do men like formulas? Why are formulas and combinations generally ineffective in capturing the hearts of our wives?

Every married couple develops a system of signals that indicate one spouse is interested in sexual activity. Maybe a man brushes his teeth and shaves at bedtime. Perhaps a woman wears a negligee to bed, instead of her flannel granny gown. There may be things spouses say or ways they approach one another in bed that signal one or both desires sexual intimacy.

Husbands and wives need to know one another's signals. Men are inclined to look for a prescribed set of behaviors that can be repeated to arouse their wives. But women aren't like safes whose combinations you learn and remember. Both marriage partners should approach moments of sexual intimacy as unique and varied opportunities to express love and give pleasure. Again, direct and sensitive communication is the key.

Embracing the Truth
15-20 MINUTES

He Says ... She Says

We looked at the fourth chapter of Song of Songs in Session One, and we discussed the sexual longing happy marriage partners have for one another. This time, we'll consider what things appealed to Solomon and his bride individually about their first sexual encounter— things that made it "good" in each of their eyes.

[HUSBAND] 12 My sister, my bride, [you are] a locked garden—a locked garden and a sealed spring. 13 Your branches are a paradise of pomegranates with choicest fruits, henna with nard—14 nard and saffron, calamus and cinnamon, with all the trees of frankincense, myrrh and aloes, with all the best spices. 15 [You are] garden spring, a well of flowing water streaming from Lebanon.

[WIFE] *16 Awaken, north wind—come, south wind. Blow on my garden, and spread the fragrance of its spices. Let my love come to his garden and eat its choicest fruits.*

SONG OF SONGS 4:12-16

1. How did Solomon demonstrate his understanding that his bride desired romance and tenderness to prepare her to enjoy fully their sexual encounter (4:12-15)?

2. How did Solomon's bride show that she realized her husband's desire for responsiveness from her to make their sexual encounter fulfilling to him (verse 16)?

3. Leaving out the details, how would your husband or wife describe "good sex"? How could you be more considerate of your lover's preferences?

Generally, a woman will define "good sex" as physically satisfying and emotionally rewarding. She wants romance and tenderness to be vital parts of the sexual experience. A man typically will define "good sex" as a physically satisfying sexual encounter during which his wife responds assertively.

This also tends to mean that men find sexual activity exhilarating. Their senses are quickly heightened and they carry sensory memories away from sexual encounters. Unfortunately, some married women find themselves engaging in sexual acts for which they aren't fully prepared. Some of these encounters are acts of loving service, but some may be unpleasant. Husbands and wives need to be committed to providing one another "good" sexual experiences on one another's terms. This becomes possible when marriage partners know one another well and communicate openly about sexual matters.

♥ Connecting

Much of what you thought about and even discussed in this session is very personal. Our "Connecting" time will help strengthen our group relationships, which will play an important role in encouraging all of us to follow through on the things we've considered.

1. What is your opinion of the frankness about sexuality in the Song of Songs passages we've discussed in the first three *Turning Up the Heat* sessions? Are you comfortable or uncomfortable with this level of explicitness?

2. Why do you think God included such a book in the Bible? Who should be encouraged to read and study it?

3. How can couples who have never talked much about what they enjoy in their sexual encounters begin to open up discussions? If you said to your spouse, "Let's talk about the way we make love," what response would you want? What kind of response would you absolutely not want?

4. How do you think you need to be more sensitive to your spouse as a microwave or a Crock Pot™?

Record group prayer requests, and pray regularly for them between now and the next session. Pray together now for each couple in the group that they will grow in understanding and love for one another.

Prayer Requests:

Taking It Home

LEADER: "Taking It Home" this week features "Questions to Take to Your Heart" and another couple's activity. Encourage everyone to complete both activities before the next session.

Learning to rekindle romance and passion takes thought and effort. The questions you take to your heart will help you evaluate your own feelings and motivations. The "Date Night" will give you an opportunity to enjoy some extended time with your spouse.

(1) Questions to Take to Your Heart on page 44

(2) A Date Night on page 45

LEADER: Have each couple set a date, time, and location for the "Date Night" … right now before you close your session.

When? _____ Where? _____

SNEAK PEEK
Next time we meet, we will turn our attention to some practical issues of how to meet our lover's sexual needs.

QUESTIONS TO TAKE TO YOUR HEART

It's likely that you are reacting to "A Combustible Mixture" something like this: "This is getting way too personal, or I could never talk about this with my spouse." Take whatever concerns you have about what you should do in response to this study, and ask your heart these questions.

Use this introspective time to grapple with what drives your thinking and behavior. Dig for what you really believe in the deep recesses of your heart about God, yourself, your spouse, and the world in which you live. Be sure to record your thoughts and feelings.

✦ How do I really feel about the level of openness with my spouse discussed in this study? Where did these feelings come from?

✦ What's preventing me from fully appreciating the differences in my spouse and focusing on meeting his or her needs romantically and sexually?

DATE NIGHT

Before the next *Turning Up the Heat* session, plan a dynamic date. Choose a seasonal activity you both enjoy: walking, skating, cycling, bowling, tennis, pool, skiing, swimming, boating, etc. Be sure to focus on the cooperative rather than the competitive aspects of what you choose to do together. Make a point of ensuring that your spouse feels successful at what you do together. Pay particular attention to your husband's or wife's movements and skills. If you have any tendency to be critical of your spouse's athleticism, banish that from your perceptions for this event and just enjoy being together physically.

At the end of your "Date Night," hold hands and give thanks to God for the physical relationship He has given you in marriage. Ask Him to bless your efforts to enhance your romance and passion.

SCRIPTURE NOTES

COLOSSIANS 3:18-19

3:18 submit. In Christ, this is transformed from a passive obedience to an authority to a specific application of Christ's call to put the needs and interests of others before one's own (Ephesians 5:21-24; Philippians 2:4).

JUDGES 16:4-20

16:5 tie him up, and make him helpless. The Philistines were still out for revenge, some 20 years after the first conflict between Samson and his father-in-law. They were not concerned with eliminating Samson unless they could torture and humiliate him.

16:7 seven fresh bowstrings. Samson, in his pride, tried to deceive the Philistines with "secrets" that would seem true. Since he knew the Philistines believed his strength was from a supernatural force, he repeatedly used the number seven, which was widely believed to have magical powers.

16:11 new ropes. Though the vendetta between Samson and the Philistines had been going on for some time, the Philistines had forgotten some of the details. They had tried new ropes before with terrible results (Judges 15:13-14).

16:13 mocked me all along and told me lies! Though it is difficult to feel compassion for Delilah, she was actually correct in her assessment of Samson's actions toward her. Out of his arrogant disdain for the Philistines, Samson had been playing a game with her and her people.

16:19-20 his strength left him ... the Lord had left him. Samson's strength was from the Spirit of the Lord. When he betrayed his vow, he nullified that special blessing.

16:20 he did not know. Samson did not know that when he betrayed his Nazirite vow the Lord would leave him, and he would lose his strength. Importantly, that vow had been made for him before he was ever born.

SONG OF SONGS 4:12-16

4:12 garden. A garden is full of beauty, refreshment, and sensual delight—a beautiful description of love (Song of Songs 4:16; 5:1). *Locked ... locked ... sealed.* References to the beloved's virginity before the wedding night.

4:14-15 all the best spices. The perfumed aromas were sensual and rich, and many of them were used in the temple anointing oil. The beloved desired the winds to blow her charming fragrances to her lover, drawing him to her.

4:16 Awaken. Both previous references to sexuality had insisted that love not be awakened before the wedding (2:7; 3:5). *Let my love come to his garden.* The beloved bride invited her lover to enjoy her sexual pleasures for the first time. He expressed his complete satisfaction as a result in 5:1.

Stoking the Flames

BECOMING A GIVING LOVER

In our last session, we looked at some of the practical implications of the differences between men and women in our expression of sexuality in marriage. We looked at the different things that ignite a fire in men and women. We considered the signals we send one another to indicate interest in sexual activity. Finally, we discussed what men and women tend to regard as "good sex."

In this session, we'll explore some concepts we need to keep in mind in order to become a giving lover. This art requires sensitivity and commitment to our mate's happiness and well-being.

Breaking the Ice 10-15 MINUTES

LEADER: These "Breaking the Ice" questions invite group members to look back at their lives and share their stories. To some degree our ability to be intimate in marriage springs from our intimacy skills in friendships. Choose any or all of the questions that fit your group.

1. Who was your best friend when you were in grade school? How would you describe the level of intimacy in that friendship?

   ○ We talked about everything. Nothing was too personal.
   ○ We chattered endlessly about the surface details of kids' stuff.
   ○ We gossiped and talked cruelly about other kids.
   ○ We joked around and made fun of everyone and everything.
   ○ We didn't talk much. We just did things together.
   ○ Other: _____ .

2. During which period of your life did you have the most intimate friendships? Why do you think that was so?

   ○ Childhood   ○ As a 30-something
   ○ High school   ○ Now
   ○ College   ○ Other: _____
   ○ As a 20-something

3. Tell about a time when you tried to be someone's friend and that person rejected you. Why do you think that person didn't want to be your friend?

LEADER: Encourage each person to share a key insight from "A Question to Take to Your Heart" or the "Date Night." This should only take a couple of minutes each, but allow a little more time if someone has something inspiring to share. Affirm couples who put a lot of energy into their active date.

4. How did your "Taking It Home" activities go? How did your active "Date Night" turn out? Is there anything you'd like to share as you searched your heart this week?

Discovering the Truth

25-30 MINUTES

LEADER: Consider showing scenes from **Field of Dreams** to lead into this discussion. In each section of "Discovering the Truth," ask various group members to read the Bible passages. Be sure to leave at least 15 minutes for the "Connecting" segment at the end of your session.

Toward the end of the movie *Field of Dreams*, Ray Kinsella got upset when he didn't get to go into the cornfield with the ghostly baseball players of the past. He protested at length about how much he had sacrificed and worked to make the ball field a reality. He concluded proudly, "And not once did I ask, 'What's in it for me?' "

Shoeless Joe Jackson replied, "What are you saying, Ray?"

Ray sputtered, "I'm saying, ... 'What's in it for me?' "

Shoeless Joe answered, "Ray, do you think this is about you?"

In the end, Ray discovered that his field of dreams wasn't about Shoeless Joe and the other legends of the game, not about himself, but about his father John Kinsella. Ray, who regretted so many angry, selfish encounters with his dad, found reconciliation on a baseball diamond just this side of heaven at the edge of a cornfield in Iowa.

Too often, we approach the sexual relationship of our marriage asking, "What's in it for me?" The surprising thing about truly satisfactory sex is that it isn't about me and my satisfaction. It becomes truly great when it's about meeting and satisfying my spouse's needs.

Be Available

In the seventh chapter of 1 Corinthians, the Apostle Paul began answering some questions the Corinthian church had asked about sex. Apparently, some in that church were teaching that truly spiritual people, if they got married at all, didn't experience the fleshly desires that prompted sexual intercourse. Such teaching reflected a strand of Greek philosophy that exalted the human spirit and looked down on the body. In keeping with the Old Testament view that body and spirit together are God's creation, Paul treated married sexuality as a noble activity with important spiritual ramifications.

> ³ A husband should fulfill his marital duty to his wife, and likewise a wife to her husband. ⁴ A wife does not have authority over her own body, but her husband does. Equally, a husband does not have authority over his own body, but his wife does. ⁵ Do not deprive one another — except when you agree, for a time, to devote yourselves to prayer. Then come together again; otherwise, Satan may tempt you because of your lack of self-control.
>
> 1 CORINTHIANS 7:3-5

LEADER: Discuss as many discovery questions as time permits. The strongest application questions appear in the "Embracing the Truth" section, but this section also has some application questions. It will help to highlight in advance the questions you don't want to miss.

Be familiar with the Scripture Notes at the end of this session to help clarify any issues. There are additional tips and helps in the Leader's Notes that begin on page 95.

1. If you were looking for a more contemporary and appealing expression than "marital duty" (1 Corinthians 7:3), what might you suggest? Why is meeting each other's needs relationally and sexually so important?

2. What are some ways the idea of authority over your spouse's body (verse 4) could be abused in either direction?

3. What benefits does this concept of authority over your spouse's body bring to marriage? How is sex enhanced by mutual respect and consideration for one another?

4. What do you suppose are some of Satan's attacks and lies that he uses when a husband and wife refrain from sexual contact for a long period of time? What will be the result of these?

5. What does it mean to be available to our spouses? In what ways do men and women at times make themselves unavailable or at least communicate distance?

"Be available" summarizes 1 Corinthians 7:3-5 pretty well. Husbands should be available to satisfy the romantic and sexual needs of their wives, and wives should be available to satisfy the romantic and sexual needs of their husbands. The idea of availability doesn't mean marriage partners are sexual vending machines for each other. Sexuality is the complex interaction we've described in the first three sessions of *Turning Up the Heat*. Availability refers to glad willingness to respond to your mate's appropriate overtures.

We'll consider boundaries in Session 5, but the starting point for satisfying sexual relations is *availability*. No woman likes to look at a newspaper or football game on TV where her husband's face should be when she wants to connect with his heart. No man likes to feel he has spent an evening wooing his wife only to have all his signals ignored and to end up frustrated in bed looking at her back as she reads a romance novel.

There are all kinds of legitimate reasons why marital encounters don't develop as we want them to. All relational moments reflect a balance of mutual desires and needs. Basic to them all, however, is the essential desire on both spouses' parts to be available to each other.

Be Considerate

Sexuality is so close to the core of our identity as men and women that our egos get very involved. In spite of our best intentions, we can be pretty self-centered people. It's hard to overstate the need for kindness, gentleness, and courtesy in our sexual relationships with our spouses. The Apostle Paul emphasizes the true nature of love in his first letter to the Corinthians.

> [4] *Love is patient; love is kind. Love does not envy; is not boastful; is not conceited;* [5] *does not act improperly; is not selfish; is not provoked; does not keep a record of wrongs;* [6] *finds no joy in unrighteousness, but rejoices in the truth;* [7] *bears all things, believes all things, hopes all things, endures all things.*
>
> 1 CORINTHIANS 13:4-7

6. What attitudes and emotions tend to be operating when a spouse is inconsiderate and demanding about sexual activity? Where could these attitudes lead?

7. In what ways can a quiet, uncomplaining spouse also be violating the standards of 1 Corinthians 13:4-7?

8. Which of these qualities of love do you think is most important in romance and intimacy? Explain.

9. Why might consideration prompt constraint? Why might it prompt generosity? What are some ways that constraint and generosity might play out in the sexual arena?

Consideration is on the other side of the coin from availability. Your spouse may be available to you, but you need to be considerate in the demands you place on that availability.

Being considerate does not make sissies out of men or doormats out of women. Consideration in sexual behavior is an application of the fruit of the Spirit to that area of life: specifically peace, patience, kindness, gentleness, and self-control. Consideration takes into account that the mother of an infant is often sleep-deprived and exhausted. Consideration recognizes that a husband facing a crisis at work may be too stressed to romance his wife.

That's the *constraint* side of consideration. Consideration also prompts *generosity*. A wife may engage more because she knows he desires her than because she desires him. A husband may forego sex in favor of holding, caressing, and talking with his wife in bed, because she enjoys that. Such consideration grows out of thorough knowledge of your partner in marriage.

![road icon] Embracing the Truth
10-15 MINUTES

Be Daring

Perhaps it seems unexpected to you that the Bible, which calls for sexual self-control before marriage, should encourage sexual self-expression within marriage. However, that is the case. This passage from the Song of Songs occurs as Solomon and his bride are reconciling after a conflict that caused them to part in anger.

> [CHORUS] *¹ Where has your love gone most beautiful of women? Which way has he turned? We will seek him for you.*
> [WIFE] *² My love has gone down to his garden, to beds of spices, to feed in the gardens and gather lilies. ³ I am my love's and my love is mine; he feeds among the lilies.*
> [HUSBAND] *⁴ You are as beautiful as Tirzah, my darling, lovely as Jerusalem, awe-inspiring as an army with banners. ⁵ Turn your eyes away from me, for they captivate me.*
>
> SONG OF SONGS 6:1-5A

1. Remember that the "garden" is used throughout the Song to refer to sexual delights. What confidence did this wife have concerning her husband's desire for her and his willingness to reconcile (verse 2)?

2. What was the basis of Solomon's reconciliation with his lover in the aftermath of their misunderstanding (verses 3 and 5)?

3. How was Solomon daring in his love to his wife (verses 4-5)? How was his beloved daring in her love for her husband (verse 3)? How do you think their acts of daring fit the needs of the other?

When we read the Song of Songs, we must conclude that Solomon was daring in using romantic words to share his heart with his beloved, and she was daring in the way she abandoned herself to him physically. The amazing thing is that each was daring in precisely the way the other wanted. What woman wouldn't want to be admired and treated special by her husband? What man wouldn't want his wife to respond assertively to lovemaking?

♡ Connecting   15 MINUTES

Intimacy is an art rather than a science, because intimacy isn't achieved by mechanically following the steps in a formula. A husband and wife achieve intimacy by paying attention to the unique nuances of one another's personalities and bodies. They commit themselves to pleasing the other. We can all achieve intimacy if we have enough desire, courage, and love to learn the art. Unfortunately, most of us probably quit being daring shortly after we got married, and put our love life on "cruise control."

LEADER: Use the following exercise to help each couple connect individually. Ask each couple to find a quiet corner where they can discuss the following questions. Put group members who came without spouses to discuss these topics together, or allow them time to think through these questions on their own.

NOTE: For this "Connecting" time, couples need to find a quiet corner to discuss these more personal questions. Your leader will call you back together in about 10 minutes.

1. In what kinds of settings and situations do you feel most open to intimacy with your husband or wife?

2. In what kinds of settings and situations do you feel least open to intimacy with your husband or wife?

3. If a married couple wants to experiment with a new sexual practice to be more daring, should they talk about it first or just dive in? Explain your response.

Men who once wrote love letters and spoke "sweet nothings" can't even pick out an anniversary card. Women who thrilled to kisses and embraces during courtship become passive sexual partners with the passage of time. These symptoms indicate romance and sexual intimacy have become numbingly routine. It truly is time to rekindle that romance and passion.

4. Share one time with your husband or wife when you felt the romance ... the intimacy ... the passion. Then share one way that you wish he or she would be more daring in the romance or intimacy department.

If your spouse chooses to become a little daring (or a lot) in response to this session, express your appreciation (Note: saying, "It's about time" is not exactly appreciative or motivating). Reciprocate. Be daring yourself.

LEADER: After 10 minutes, call the group back together to close your session.

Record group prayer requests, and pray regularly for them between now and the next session. Pray together today that each if the marriages represented in your group will become more romantic and passionate.

Prayer Requests:

🏠 Taking It Home

LEADER: "Taking It Home" this week provides "A Question to Take to God" and a formal couple's date. Be sure group members realize the level of formality for "Date Night" is up to each couple. Encourage everyone to complete this before the next session.

This session, "Stoking the Flames," raised more intensely personal issues. "A Question to Take to God" gives you an opportunity to seek God's perspective on some barely conscious values that influence your sexual attitudes. The "Date Night" activity should help to enrich your relationship with by practicing being "available" and "considerate." For any acts of "daring," you're on your own ...

(1) A Question to Take to God on page 56

(2) A Date Night on page 57

LEADER: Have each couple set a date, time, and location for the "Date Night" ... right now before you close your session.

When? _____ Where? _____

SNEAK PEEK
Next time we meet, our focus will be on determining the boundaries for which sexual practices are acceptable and which aren't in a couple's marriage.

A Question to Take to God

All of us want to have sexually well-adjusted marriages, but most of us probably can identify areas where we don't do as well as we wish we did. Husbands and wives bring baggage into their marriages packed with misinformation, bad experiences, personal doubts and fears, insecurities, emotional issues, etc. All of these things hinder healthy sexual relationships. At a time when you can sit quietly and focus on the nudging of God's Spirit, ask Him this question and seek to understand His heart and your own. Be sure to keep a journal of the insights you gain from your times with God.

- God, what baggage am I still dragging around that's negatively affecting my ability to be "available," " considerate," and "daring" for my spouse?

- Where did this baggage come from? What was the source? Is there anything You want to say to me to clear up any lies I'm believing?

DATE NIGHT

So far, our three "Date Night" activities have been pretty casual, unless you ate at a nice restaurant after Session One. Before the next *Turning Up the Heat* session, plan and carry out a date for which you have to dress up. Make it a play, a concert, or some other formal event other than dinner. You can make this as elegant as you like, depending on your preferences and resources, but the point isn't spending a lot of money. The point is to treat your mate with consideration, courtesy, and dignity.

Husbands, open doors, hold chairs, and otherwise honor your wife. Wives, respond graciously to your husband's attentions. Compliment one another and focus on pleasing one another by means of the formality of the occasion. In this way, you practice availability and consideration in other than sexual ways. That is important too.

At the end of your "Date Night," spend some time talking about what you enjoyed about the formality of your evening. Thank your spouse for making your evening special. Be as specific as you can.

SCRIPTURE NOTES

1 CORINTHIANS 7:3-5

7:3 marital duty. While it's true that in the experience of many married couples the man wants sexual relations more often than the woman, that isn't always the case. Husbands need to understand the sexual desires of their wives and respect them. However, mutual delight is an important goal for couples to discuss and pursue rather than pursuing sexual activity primarily to satisfy themselves.

7:4 have authority. The Greek verb literally means "to have rights over" or "to have exclusive claim to." Marriage partners do not have exclusive individual rights to determine what sexual activities they will engage in. Their partners do. Accordingly, such decisions must be made mutually, with each partner giving preference to the other.

7:5 deprive. Literally, "rob." For one partner to opt out of sexual relations under the guise of spirituality is a form of robbery. However, this verse is not a "club" to use on a disinterested mate. It's a warning about the spiritual dangers of sexual dysfunction. It is also a challenge for women to learn how to respond to their husbands, and for men to learn how to show tender physical affection to their wives. Abstinence is allowed under two conditions: both partners agree, and it is for a limited time. *prayer.* The purpose of such abstinence is prayer. *lack of self-control.* Paul assumes that a couple would not be married in the first place if they did not feel any sexual desire, and thus they ought to fulfill such desires legitimately, lest they be tempted to fall into adultery.

1 CORINTHIANS 13:4-7

13:4 patient. This word describes patience with people (not circumstances). It characterizes the person who is slow to anger (long-suffering) despite provocation. *kind.* The loving person does good to others. *not envy.* The loving person does not desire what others have, nor begrudge them their possessions. *not boastful.* The loving person is self-effacing, not a braggart. *not conceited.* Literally, not "puffed up." The loving person neither feels others to be inferior nor looks down on them.

13:5 not selfish. Loving people not only do not insist on their rights, but will give up their due for the sake of others. *not provoked.* Loving people are not easily angered by others; they are not touchy. *does not keep a record of wrongs.* The verb is an accounting term, and the image is of a ledger sheet on which wrongs received are recorded. The loving person forgives and leaves wrongs in the past.

13:6 finds no joy in unrighteousness. Loving people do not rejoice when others fail or enjoy pointing out the wrong in others. *rejoices in the truth.* Paul shifted back to the positive after a string of negative traits of love.

13:7 bears all things. Literally, "to put a cover over." The loving person is concerned with how to shelter other people from harm. *believes all things.* Love always trusts; it never loses faith. *hopes.* Our love continually looks forward because of God's love. *endures all things.* Love keeps loving despite hardship.

6:1 We. This verse is spoken by "the young women of Jerusalem" (2:7; 3:5; 5:16; 8:4) who function as a chorus in this love poem (5:9; 6:10,13; 8:5). They offer to help the beloved find her husband with whom she has had a misunderstanding.

6:2-3 My love. The bride speaks erotically in these two verses as she welcomes Solomon after their disagreement. *gather lilies.* Imaginative language that possibly portrays the lover as a gazelle (2:7) nibbling on the alluring lilies in the exotic garden, thus enjoying intimate moments with his beloved.

6:4 You are. Solomon responds to his bride romantically instead of focusing on what had separated them. *Tirzah.* Tirzah was the capitol of Israel's northern kingdom, known for its grand architecture.

6:5 Turn your eyes. The lover is captivated by the deep love he sees through his beloved's eyes—and it is almost too wonderful to bear (4:9).

Fire Safety

LOVING BOUNDARIES DEEPEN INTIMACY

In Session Four, we discussed stoking the flames of intimacy. We considered how intimacy is an art to be learned and thrives in a romantic atmosphere. *Availability* recognizes our mate's right to sexual relations. *Consideration* approaches sexuality gently and courteously. A *daring* spirit embraces and explores the essentially sensuous nature of sex in marriage.

In this session, we'll explore a healthy concept of boundaries that will protect a marriage from the outside and foster safety and security at home. At first glance, boundaries seem opposed to a daring spirit, but they aren't. The mutual aspect of sexuality merely clarifies what both are ready to dare at this stage of their relationship. Mutually agreed boundaries create a safer environment for "turning up the heat."

Breaking the Ice   10 - 15 MINUTES

LEADER: The "Breaking the Ice" questions invite group members to remember some experiences they've had with life boundaries. Choose any or all that you feel will benefit your group. Be sure to keep the discussion light as you begin your session.

1. Highway speed limits are boundaries that people have widely differing perspectives on. It's true confession time – which perspective best describes your view?

   ○ If they didn't want me to go that fast, why did they make put those speeds on the speedometer?
   ○ It's the law, so why do all these clowns think they can ignore it?
   ○ Speed limits were designed for people who don't drive as well as I do.
   ○ I push a little beyond the speed limit because that's the "real" boundary.
   ○ I go the speeds I think are safe, but I keep my eyes open for law enforcement
   ○ They make the rules, so if I break them I pay the consequences.
   ○ Do we have speed limits?

2. Identify a rule or boundary your parents placed on you that you thought ridiculous when you were 15? How do you feel about it now?

3. Tell about a time when you overstepped a boundary and wished you hadn't.

LEADER: Encourage each person to share a key insight from "A Question to Take to God" or the "Date Night." This should only take a couple of minutes each, but allow a little more time if someone has something inspiring to share. Affirm individuals who gained are beginning to connect with their hearts and with God.

4. What did you learn from the "Taking It Home" activities? Are there any insights God revealed to you about your baggage? What did you enjoy or learn from the formal aspect of your "Date Night?"

Discovering the Truth

15-20 MINUTES

LEADER: In each section of "Discovering the Truth," ask a different group member to read the Bible passage or passages. Be sure to leave at least 20 minutes this time for the "Connecting" segment.

Who Needs Boundaries?

What would happen if property boundaries were non-existent? Imagine a neighbor tearing out a garden you planted so he could ride his dirt bike in that area. Consider a neighbor barging into your kitchen anytime she needed supplies for cooking dinner. Picture your response to the family up the street taking your big screen TV so they could really enjoy watching their favorite movies and sports teams.

LEADER: Discuss as many discovery questions as time permits. It will help to highlight in advance the questions you don't want to miss. Application questions are included here and in "Embracing the Truth."

Be familiar with the Scripture Notes at the end of this session to help clarify any issues. Check the Leader's Notes that begin on page 95.

1. How would you feel in these scenarios if it were you and your property boundaries were not respected?

Boundaries are vital in relationships too. Drs. Cloud and Townsend in their classic book *Boundaries* (Zondervan, 2002) say boundaries "define *what is me* and *what is not me*." A boundary is "*where I end and someone else begins.*" God created boundaries and His instruction manual for life discusses them a lot.

> *[Jesus words to His followers ...] Here I am! I stand at the door and knock. If anyone hears my voice and opens the door, I will come in and eat with him and he with me.*
>
> REVELATION 3:20 (NIV)

> *[Jesus' invitation ...]* 7 *"Ask, and it will be given to you; seek, and you will find; knock, and it will be opened to you.* 8 *"For everyone who asks receives, and he who seeks finds, and to him who knocks it will be opened.*
>
> MATTHEW 7:7-8 (NASB)

> *[Jesus' offer ...]* 28 *"Come to me, all of you who are weary and burdened, and I will give you rest.* 29 *Take up my yoke upon me and learn from me, for I am gentle and humble in heart, and you will find rest for your souls.*
>
> Matthew 11:28-29 (NIV)

> *"I am the bread of life," Jesus told them. "No one who comes to Me will ever be hungry, and no one who believes in Me will ever be thirsty again."*
>
> JOHN 6:35

2. What sense do Jesus' words give you about how He views and treats our personal boundaries?

[2] Carry one another's burdens; in this way you will fulfill the law of Christ. ... [5] each person will have to carry his own load.

GALATIANS 6:2,5

[7] For whatever a man sows he will also reap .... [10] Therefore, as we have opportunity, we must work for the good of all, especially for those who belong to the household of faith.

GALATIANS 6:7,10

3. How do you see the apparently opposing views in Galatians 6 about responsibility and boundaries coming together? Where do our responsibilities end and others' begin?

God has boundaries within the Trinity and has established and honors boundaries with us. He won't force us to accept Him or the gifts He has for us. He respects our separateness from Him and our freedom of choice even though He longs to be united with us. He created people with the same need for living united in community, and yet each person is meant to be responsible for himself and honor the boundaries of others. Let's look at boundaries that protect and honor our marriages.

Marriage Boundaries

There's a prevalent view that suggests limiting yourself to one sexual partner for life has to be boring. Variety, these proponents insist, can only be found with multiple partners. God paints a totally different picture of intimacy and excitement in a lifelong marriage. In order enjoy marriage the way God intended it, we must protect it.

18 Let your fountain be blessed, and take pleasure in the wife of your youth. 19 A loving doe, a graceful fawn — let her breasts always satisfy you; be lost in her love forever.

PROVERBS 5:18-19

Marriage should be honored by all, and the marriage bed kept pure, because God will judge the adulterer and all the sexually immoral.

HEBREWS 13:4

[Regarding sex outside marriage ...] 27 Can a man scoop fire into his lap without his clothes being burned? 28 Can a man walk on hot coals without his feet being scorched?

PROVERBS 6:27-28

4. How can your fountain be blessed (Proverbs 5:18-19) as you focus on deepening intimacy in marriage over a lifetime together?

5. Proverbs 6:27-28 refers to sex outside of marriage as scooping "fire" into our laps? What are some consequences that are likely for somebody who chooses to ignore God's instructions about keeping the marriage bed pure?

6. What are some hedges of protection (physically, emotionally, spiritually) that we need to plant around our marriages to keep us far away from the possibility of infidelity?

Embracing the Truth

15-20 MINUTES

LEADER: This section dives right into the topic of loving boundaries and focuses on helping couples begin to integrate what they have learned from the Bible into their own marriages.

Bedroom Boundaries: Avoid Steam-Rolling

Husbands and wives are supposed to be different. Invariably we find that we have different ideas about what sexual activities are enjoyable and even acceptable. Each married couple has to discover the boundaries that apply to their relationship. Differences can add spice to live, but they can also cause struggles. God set up the system to help us grow in maturity and love.

> *3 A husband should fulfill his marital duty to his wife, and likewise a wife to her husband. 4 A wife does not have authority over her own body, but her husband does. Equally, a husband does not have authority over his own body, but his wife does.*
> 1 CORINTHIANS 7:3-4

> *Now the Lord is the Spirit; and where the Spirit of the Lord is, there is freedom.*
> 2 CORINTHIANS 3:17

> *18 There is no fear in love; instead, perfect love drives out fear, because fear involves punishment. So the one who fears has not reached perfection in love.*
> 1 JOHN 4:18-19

1. How does the equal authority of both spouses over each other's bodies (1 Corinthians 7:2-4) assure access to sexual relations and also prevent abuse of that access?

2. What do these words about "freedom" and "perfect love driving out fear" have to do with honoring boundaries and what goes on in our bedrooms?

3. What do you suppose will happen to the sexual life of a marriage when one partner demands activities without regard for the other's feelings?

Bedroom Boundaries: Avoid Unhealthy Self-Protection

God designed balance into everything including our marriages. Our marriage boundaries should be mutually agreed upon. Problems hit when one spouse or the other holds all or the majority of the power.

Stop depriving one another, except by agreement for a time, so that you may devote yourselves to prayer, and come together again so that Satan will not tempt you because of your lack of self-control.

1 CORINTHIANS 7:5 (NASB)

[1] Therefore if there is any encouragement in Christ, if there is any consolation of love, if there is any fellowship of the Spirit, if any affection and compassion, [2] make my joy complete by being of the same mind, maintaining the same love, united in spirit, intent on one purpose. [3] Do nothing from selfishness or empty conceit, but with humility of mind regard one another as more important than yourselves; [4] do not merely look out for your own personal interests, but also for the interests of others.

PHILIPPIANS 2:1-4 (NASB)

4. What do you expect will happen to the sexual life of a marriage in which one partner consistently refuses the sexual advances of the other? When is it okay according to 1 Corinthians 7:5 to veto sexual advances and how should this be done?

5. What are some ways that husbands and wives can "deprive on another"? What might be some causes for this?

6. If a couple carries the attitudes of Philippians 2:1-4 into the bedroom, how might that affect their romance and lovemaking? How might it affect the way determine and treat boundaries?

Some boundaries may be excessively limiting; others reasonable and appropriate. If there is disagreement, try talking with close godly friends, a pastor, or a counselor to gauge your boundaries. Boundaries typically expand as a relationship develops. If we look out for the interests of the other, we won't violate his or her sense of security for the sake of selfish pleasure nor deprive each other out of selfishness, unhealthy self-protection, or fear.

The message in 1 Corinthians 7:2-5 is wonderfully balanced. The wife's body belongs to the husband, and the husband's body belongs to the wife. Neither can demand anything distressing of the other. They should want to agree in order to please the other. Discomfort about what is being asked is a good reason to say, "No." However, any veto needs to be for a good reason and communicated with love and honor to avoid shutting a spouse down.

NOTE ON ABUSE: Most husbands and wives are considerate of each other and willing to work at enhancing romance and intimacy. However, there are occasional situations in which there's abuse in a marriage. A Christian abuser may even justify behaviors with a twisted interpretation of 1 Corinthians 7:4. When boundaries are violated, it's important to seek out a pastor or Christian counselor sensitive to and experienced in issues of abuse.

♥ Connecting

20 MINUTES

LEADER: Use this "Connecting" time to develop a sense of community in your group, as you continue to grow closer and build one another up. Encourage everyone to join in and to be open with one another, but allow members who don't wish to share on a particular topic to pass.

Knowing and respecting the boundaries of what our spouse feels to be great sex is an aspect of intimacy that communicates our deepest understanding and love for our marriage partner. A group session isn't the time to talk about specific sexual boundaries of our marriages, but it gives us an opportunity to share our thoughts about the value of such boundaries.

Each for the Other

In the Song of Songs, some time into the marriage of Solomon and his beloved, we find them setting out on a romantic journey. Their outing was in the spring – the same as their courtship. (2:11-12). Spring is symbolic of rekindled love and romance. In the beloved's words to and about Solomon, we find an indication of the spirit that characterized the romance between this woman and her husband.

[11] *Come, my love, let's go to the field; let's spend the night among the henna blossoms.* *[12]* *Let's go early to the vineyards; let's see if the vine has budded, if the blossom has opened, if the pomegranates are in bloom. There I will give you my love.* *[13]* *The mandrakes give off a fragrance, and at our doors is every delicacy — new as well as old. I have treasured them up for you, my love.*

[1] *If only I could treat you like my brother, one who nursed at my mother's breasts, I would find you in public and kiss you, and no one would scorn me.* *[2]* *I would lead you, I would take you, to the house of my mother who taught me. I would give you spiced wine to drink from my pomegranate juice.*

[3] *His left hand is under my head, and his right hand embraces me.*

SONG OF SONGS 7:11—8:3

NOTE: *Public expressions of affection between husbands and wives were forbidden in Hebrew culture. A woman could publicly kiss her father or brother. In her passion, Solomon's beloved wanted to break conventions.*

1. What does this wife do in approaching her husband to avoid the extremes of busting through boundaries and of unhealthy self-protection?

2. Are you surprised to see this model wife initiating romance and sex? Explain. Why do you think she felt free to share her spontaneous and intimate ideas with her husband?

3. What do you think is meant in Songs 7:13 by "every delicacy — new as well as old"? What are some ways Solomon's beloved approaches their romance with a spirit of spontaneity, variety, and creativity?

4. This encounter depicts sexual play – not marital duty. How do marriages fall into routine and dullness? Do you think there's any relation between loss of creativity in other areas of marriage and a couple's lovemaking?

5. What are some ways that couples might add freshness to their lovemaking while honoring mutually agreed boundaries?

At the core of setting loving boundaries is that both marital partners actively engage in defining their parameters. The happiest sexual relationships between husbands and wives are characterized by spontaneity, variety, and creativity within the context of knowing what each marriage partner enjoys and offers.

The secret to avoiding dullness and routine is committing to discover one another over a lifetime. The wife in the Song of Songs suggested lovemaking outdoors (7:11-12). She imagined expressing her affection for her husband publicly in ways that would have shocked her culture (8:1).

When husbands and wives are well-versed in their lover's likes and dislikes, they can exercise creativity in using the tried and true "old" practices and in imagining new ways of pleasing one another. God leaves the door wide open for great freedom within mutually agreed boundaries.

Record group prayer requests, and pray regularly for them between now and the next session. Pray that couples in the group will understand and benefit from their mutually agreed upon sexual boundaries.

Prayer Requests:

🏠 Taking It Home

LEADER: The "Taking It Home" activities provide husbands and wives with "A Question to Take to God" and an at-home "Date Night." Encourage everyone to complete both projects before the next session.

It is important for any couple seeking intimacy in their marriage to agree upon unselfish and loving boundaries. It's vital for achieving intimacy. Sometimes we get caught up in our own agenda for shaping our marriage into what we want and forget to consider fully what our spouse wants as well. We know God wants us to show honor and put our husband's or wife's interests ahead of our own, but it's hard to do on a day-to-day basis. Let the "Taking It Home" activities keep the subject of loving boundaries in the front of your mind in the days ahead.

(1) A Question to Take to God on page 71

(2) A Date Night on page 72

LEADER: Have each couple set a date, time, and location for the "Date Night" … right now before you close your session.

When? _____ Where? _____

SNEAK PEEK

Next time we meet, we conclude our study by considering how our sexual relationship as husband and wife nourishes other aspects of our marriage.

A QUESTION TO TAKE TO GOD

It's easy to let negative feelings about a spouse build up in private corners of our heart. Many of us find our mate's sexual desires or limitations puzzling or frustrating. Often we're more interested in changing our lover than understanding him or her. Ask God to help you redirect your heart from your negative feelings to your husband's or wife's needs. True love in marriage will never be an "easy street." At the core of love is always commitment to follow Jesus' model and commands to love regardless of feelings and circumstances.

PRAYER: God who created my marriage partner, give me insights into my beloved's heart and show me the value his or her differences bring into my life.

✚ Do I tend to steamroll or dishonor the boundaries of my spouse? If so, why? What's really behind my attitudes and actions?

✚ Do I tend to be more self-protective or unwilling to expand my boundaries for my spouse—adding variety, spontaneity, and creativity? If so, why? What's really behind my attitudes and actions?

DATE NIGHT

Before the final *Turning Up the Heat* session, enjoy a "Date Night" at home playing your favorite games. Choose from board games, word games, video games, card games, table games, etc. Order in a pizza, or load up on chips and snack foods. As with your dynamic date from Session Three, focus on the social rather than the competitive aspects of the games. The point of the evening is to enjoy time together and to talk about anything and everything as the games give structure to the evening.

If you have small children, you may want to swap childcare with another couple with kids from your *Turning Up the Heat* group. That way your children will have adult supervision and you and your spouse can enjoy uninterrupted time together.

Sexual boundaries is a serious topic, and Session Five was a heavy small-group session. Keep your "Date Night" light and enjoyable. If you do want to share conversation related to boundaries, thank your beloved for being available to you sexually and for respecting your sexual boundaries. Remember, God has given you a gift in each other.

SCRIPTURE NOTES

REVELATION 3:20

3:20 I stand at the door and knock. Although often used to invite those without faith to Jesus, in this context the call is actually to those within the church to return to the Lord from whom they have turned away. *eat with him.* Sharing a meal was a sign of an intimate bond.

GALATIANS 6:2,5

6:2 Carry one another's burdens. Mutual burden-bearing lies at the heart of Christian fellowship and especially marriage. *burdens.* A heavy, crushing weight, which a single individual cannot carry. *law of Christ.* The law of love (5:14), which stands in sharp contrast to the Jewish Law.

6:5 load. This is not the same as the crushing burden in verse 2. Rather, the word is used to describe the small individual pack a hiker or soldier carries. This is the same word used by Jesus in Matthew 11:30 to describe the burden (load) of His yoke, signifying that each of us has a burden (load) to carry.

PROVERBS 5:18-19

5:18 fountain. Euphemism for the male sexual organ.

5:19 doe … fawn. The animal imagery depicts the young wife as graceful and, perhaps, shy.

1 JOHN 4:18-19

4:18 no fear in love. People cannot love and fear at the same moment. The love casts out the fear. *fear involves punishment.* This is the root of the fear: they think God is going to punish them. They forget that they are His forgiven children.

1 CORINTHIANS 7:3-5

See page 60 of this book.

PHILIPPIANS 2:1-4

2:1 If. In Greek, this construction assumes a positive response, for example, "If then there is any encouragement, and of course there is …

2:3 selfishness. This is the second time Paul uses this word in Philippians (1:17). It means working to advance oneself without thought for others. *conceit.* This is the only occurrence of this word in the New Testament. Translated literally, it means "vain glory" (kendoxia), which is asserting oneself over God who alone is worthy of true glory (doxia). *humility.* This was not a virtue valued by the Greeks in the first century. They considered this the attitude of a slave (that is, servility).

SONG OF SONGS 7:12–8:3

7:12 There I will give you my love. The beloved commits herself fully, offering herself to her lover.

7:13 mandrakes. These flowering herbs with a pungent fragrance were considered potent aphrodisiacs.

8:1 like my brother. Hebrew culture forbade public expressions of affection between husbands and wives. A woman could publicly kiss her brother or her father but not her husband. She would not be seen entering an empty house with her husband because that implied they would have sexual intercourse there. In her passion, Solomon's beloved wanted to break those conventions.

The Cozy Bonfire

SEXUALITY WARMS AND NOURISHES A MARRIAGE

Last time we looked at the role of boundaries in relation to sexual intimacy. We noted that while a sexual relationship flourishes in an atmosphere of spontaneity, variety, and creativity, it must be protected externally with a hedge and internally from anything demeaning to either of the marriage partners. Love always protects and always looks out for the best interests of its beloved.

We wrap up our *Turning Up the Heat* study with a session about the ways a healthy sexual relationship serves as an indicator of the overall relationship and also nourishes a marriage. Biologically, sex leads to reproduction of the human species. Emotionally, it's an expression of love and commitment. Spiritually, it's an expression our unity as a couple and praise to God who designed us to function as "one flesh."

Breaking the Ice 10 - 15 MINUTES

LEADER: These "Breaking the Ice" questions cover a variety of topics related to the themes of unity and nourishment. Use any or all of these that will help your group get started with the final session.

1. What is your favorite form of nourishment in each of these unofficial "food groups"?

   ○ Fast food
   ○ Desserts
   ○ Salty snacks
   ○ Liquid refreshment
   ○ Meat or other entrées
   ○ Fruits and veggies
   ○ Anything chocolate
   ○ Other: _____

2. What is the first club, team, or other group that you really felt a part of? What did you like about belonging?

3. Can you recall an incident in which your spouse knew what you were thinking, doing, or going to say when he or she had no explainable way of knowing? Please describe it.

LEADER: Encourage each person to share a key insight from "A Question to Take to God" or the "Date Night." This should only take a couple of minutes each, but allow a little more time if it's beneficial to the group or couple. Affirm those who share meaningful observations.

4. What did you learn from the "Taking It Home" activities? Did God reveal anything you'd like to share? What have you learned through the course of this study about the crucial role of communication in marital intimacy?

Discovering the Truth
25 - 30 MINUTES

LEADER: In each section of "Discovering the Truth," ask a different group member to read each of Bible passages. Be sure to leave at least 15 minutes for the "Connecting" segment at the end the session.

Sex Unites

Genesis 2:24 introduced the concept of man and woman designed by our Creator to unite sexually as we become "one flesh." This concept is also referred to several times in the rest of the Bible (e.g. Matthew 19:5; Mark 10:6-8; 1 Corinthians 6:16; Ephesians 5:31). We'll be looking at what Jesus had to say on this topic and what Paul wrote to the church at Corinth.

²³ And the man said: This one, at last, is bone of my bone, and flesh of my flesh; this one will be called woman, for she was taken from man. ²⁴ This is why a man leaves his father and mother and bonds with his wife, and they become one flesh.

GENESIS 2:23-24

[Jesus spoke about marriage quoting Genesis 2] ⁶ "But at the beginning of creation God 'made them male and female.' ⁷ 'For this reason a man will leave his father and mother and be united with his wife, ⁸ and the two will become one flesh.' So they are no longer two, but one."

MARK 10:6-8 (NIV)

¹⁵ Do you not know that your bodies are the members of Christ? So should I take the members of Christ and make them members of a prostitute? Absolutely not! ¹⁶ Do you not know that anyone joined to a prostitute is one body with her? For it says, The two will become one flesh. ¹⁷ But anyone joined to the Lord is one spirit with Him. ¹⁸ Flee from sexual immorality! "Every sin a person can commit is outside the body," but the person who is sexually immoral sins against his own body.

I CORINTHIANS 6:15-18

LEADER: Discuss as many discovery questions as time permits. Application questions appear in both this section and "Embracing the Truth." It helps to decide in advance questions you don't want to miss.

Be familiar with the Scripture Notes at the end of this session to help clarify any issues. There are additional tips and helps in the Leader's Notes that begin on page 95.

1. What do you suppose it meant to Adam at a heart level and a soul level that God had made Eve from his flesh and bones (Genesis 2:23)?

2. What do you think "one flesh" (Genesis 2:24; 1 Corinthians 6:16) and "no longer two, but one" (Mark 10:8) refer to? What are the implications and benefits of this for our marriages?

3. Why do you think Jesus and the Apostle Paul refer back to the "beginning of creation" (Genesis 2:23-24) when they give instructions for marriage and sex?

4. According to 1 Corinthians 6:15-18, why does sex get so complicated? What are the heart and soul-level consequences of extramarital affairs or hired sex?

God is complex and relational and He created us His image. From the Bible and our own experiences, we realize that our bodies are not separate from our minds, emotions, and spirits. Each affects the other. This is particularly true with sexual union.

Sex is more than a physical union. It goes deeper by design, merging our souls and hearts. We make a serious mistake whenever we cheapen sexual activity and treat it as mere play. Sex outside of marriage does soul damage (1 Corinthians 6:18). Instead, we should treat as special and even holy—something God created through which He deepens our relationship and also demonstrates His love and union with us.

Sex Deepens Love

In this section, we will be looking at two very different passages: one from the Song of Songs and the other from Ephesians. In the first, Solomon very frankly, if poetically through the "garden" analogy, refers to sexual relations with his wife. In the second, Paul appeals to Jesus' relationship with His church as the primary metaphor for how husbands and wives should love each other.

> [1] *I have come to my garden — my sister, my bride. I gather my myrrh with my spices. I eat my honeycomb with my honey. I drink my wine with my milk.*
> SONG OF SONGS 5:1

22 Wives, submit to your own husbands as to the Lord, 23 for the husband is head of the wife as also Christ is head of the church. He is the Savior of the body. 24 Now as the church submits to Christ, so wives should [submit] to their husbands in everything. 25 Husbands, love your wives, just as also Christ loved the church and gave Himself for her, 26 to make her holy, cleansing her in the washing of water by the word. 27 He did this to present the church to Himself in splendor, without spot or wrinkle or any such thing, but holy and blameless. 28 In the same way, husbands should love their wives as their own bodies. He who loves his wife loves himself. 29 For no one ever hates his own flesh, but provides and cares for it, just as Christ does for the church, 30 since we are members of His body. 31 For this reason a man will leave his father and mother and be joined to his wife, and the two will become one flesh.

EPHESIANS 5:22-31

5. Solomon described sex with his wife in terms of spices, sweet foods, and rich beverages (Song of Songs 5:1). What does this indicate about the meaning of the experience to him?

6. How does Ephesians 5:22-30 further illustrate the merger of physical, emotional, and spiritual in marriage?

7. What does Ephesians 5:31 mean by "leave" and by "be joined to his wife"? What significance does sexual union have to our love and commitment to each other?

8. How do you think a loving sexual relationship nourishes the hearts and souls of a husband and wife?

When a man and woman commit themselves to one another in marriage, they seal that union with a sexual connection. By that means, they give themselves wholly to one another. They become open and vulnerable in intensely sensuous ways. As their marriage progresses, as long as they keep all other channels of communication open, their sexual activity will continue to emphasize their deep personal connection with one another.

Nothing is more appropriate than for a man to hold his wife after sex and pray, "I thank You, God, for this woman who gives meaning to my life." And for her to embrace him and pray, "Father, thank You for my husband who loves me so tenderly and sweetly." It doesn't get any better than that.

Embracing the Truth
10-15 MINUTES

Sex in Marriage Pleases God

The uniform witness of various parts of the Bible is that God takes special delight in the sexual union of men and women in marriage. He created the sexual aspect of our human nature, and He had more than reproduction in mind.

> [27] *God created man in His own image, in the image of God He created him; male and female He created them.* [28] *God blessed them; and God said to them, "Be fruitful and multiply, and fill the earth, and subdue it; and rule over the fish of the sea and over the birds of the sky and over every living thing that moves on the earth." ... [31] God saw all that He had made, and behold, it was very good.*
>
> GENESIS 1:27-28, 31A (NASB)

> [3] *Your wife will be like a fruitful vine within your house, your sons, like young olive trees around your table.* [4] *In this very way the man who fears the Lord will be blessed.*
>
> PSALM 128:3-4

> *Enjoy life with the wife you love all the days of your fleeting life, which has been given to you under the sun, all your fleeting days. For that is your portion in life and in your struggle under the sun*
>
> ECCLESIASTES 9:9

[GOD] ¹ Eat, friend! Drink, be intoxicated with love!

SONG OF SONGS 5:1C

1. What do you suppose God considered "very good" about the man and woman He had created (Genesis 1:27-28a, 31a)? What did Adam and Eve's sexuality have to do with this?

2. The psalmist described a blessed man's wife as "a fruitful vine" (Psalm 128:3). How does the vine image portray childbearing? How does it portray feminine sexuality? (Remember the image of the "garden" as sexual delights in Song of Songs.)

3. How does the nature of God's blessing in Psalm 128:3-4 and the encouragement in Ecclesiastes 9:9 show about God's view of sex?

4. "Friends" refers not just to Solomon and his wife, but applies also to the readers of the book. So what does Song of Songs 5:1 express about God's attitude toward sexual passion and pleasure in our marriages?

After God created Adam and Eve and commanded them to be fruitful and multiply, He was pleased and called His creation "very good" (Genesis 1:31). He created Adam and Eve to live and relate to one another in a naked and shameless state (2:25). Every dimension of their relationship, including the sexual one, occurred naturally and harmoniously. They never disappointed or took advantage of one another in any way. Their sexual activity expressed their love, their unity, and their complete vulnerability.

Married love and sex are pleasing and good in God's eyes, even in our fallen world. God has nothing but praise for it in both the Old and New Testaments.

♥ Connecting

As we conclude our *Turning Up the Heat* study, we should commit ourselves to nurturing romance and passion in our marriages and affirm the friendships that have developed among couples in the course of this study. There aren't a lot of Bible studies about this topic or a large number of couples intentionally pursuing the sexual intimacy God wants for their marriages. May He enrich and deepen your marriage in all its dimensions.

1. What primary ideas will you take from this study and try to implement in your life?

2. How have you come to treasure and appreciate your spouse more because of *Turning Up the Heat*?

3. What was your favorite "Date Night" activity? What made it special to you?

4. How has discussing such personal issues as passion and sexuality strengthened your bond with other group members?

Record group prayer requests, and pray regularly for growing unity in the marriages of your friends. Pray also for the future direction of the group.

Prayer Requests:

🏠 Taking It Home

LEADER: The "Taking It Home" activities include "Questions to Take to Your Heart" and a "Date Night" that will encourage your group members to share their hearts with their mates.

You won't be sharing anything from this "Taking It Home" activity with your group. However, it's still important to take time in the next few days to reflect alone and with your spouse about this study on *Turning Up the Heat*.

(1) Questions to Take to Your Heart on page 83

(2) A Date Night on page 84

LEADER: Have each couple set a date, time, and location for the "Date Night" ... right now before you close your session.

When? _____ Where? _____

Other Helpful Resources:
- *The Book of Romance*, Tommy Nelson (Nelson Books, 1998)
- *The Song of Solomon Series*, Tommy Nelson (thesongofsolomon.com)
- *Boundaries*, Drs. Henry Cloud & John Townsend (Zondervan, 2002)
- *Intimate Issues*, Linda Dillow & Lorraine Pintus (Waterbrook Press, 1999)
- *Love Life for Every Married Couple*, Dr. Ed Wheat (Zondervan, 1980)
- *Rekindling the Romance*, Dennis & Barbara Rainey (Nelson Books, 2004)
- *Simply Romantic Nights*, Dennis & Barbara Rainey (FamilyLife, 2001)
- *Intended for Pleasure*, Dr. Ed & Gaye Wheat (Revell, 1997)
- *The Five Love Languages*, Gary D. Chapman (Moody, 1996)

Questions to Take to Your Heart

Sexual expression that unifies our marriages, deepens our love, and pleases God is intensely honest and vulnerable. In the beginning, Adam and Eve lived in paradise together with no barriers between them and with no shame (Genesis 2:25). Since sin entered human experience, we struggle to achieve trusting intimacy. Give yourself a significant amount of time to look deep within and examine your heart for answers to this question. Don't assume the first thoughts that come to your mind are from the inner recesses of your heart.

✣ Does our lovemaking as a couple deepen our love? Is sex enjoyable for me and for my spouse?

✣ If sex is not all it should be in our relationship, what are the barriers? What false beliefs have I embraced about myself, my spouse, God, or sex that prevent deeper unity and enjoyment for both of us?

DATE NIGHT

The final "Date Night" activity is sort of a romantic scavenger hunt and will require a tapping into your fun side. This is your mission should you choose to accept it ... Plan a trip to the shopping mall in your area with the widest selection of shops. (If you live in a rural area, you may have to drive some distance to do this or adapt the exercise to the stores along Main Street in the nearest town.) Take turns selecting stores.

Browse the aisles until the spouse who chose the shop identifies an item of merchandise that reminds him or her of some aspect of your romance or passion. That person has to explain to the other what the item represents. For instance, aftershave or a negligee might have an obvious, almost literal meaning, but a necktie or a hot water heater would need more imagination and explanation.

Have fun. Make jokes. Be serious and romantic. Reveal your heart and affirm your spouse at the same time. After an hour or so, stop at a food court or coffee shop for a snack or a meal. While you eat, each should share which item the other chose that was the most meaningful to him or her.

End your "Date Night" with expressions of love and thanks to God for His blessing in your marriage.

SCRIPTURE NOTES

GENESIS 1:27-28A, 31A; 2:23-24

1:27 male and female. Who of us is not aware of the differences between men and women? And yet, both were created in the image of God and given the responsibility to take care of the earth. In how men and women relate to each other, we are different; in how we relate to God, we are the same.

1:28 rule. God gave mankind the responsibility to rule over the world. Ruling over and subduing does not mean merely "being the boss" nor is it an invitation to exploitation. Instead, mankind's "rule" over the world means nurturing it with creativity and care.

2:23 woman ... taken from man. In Hebrew "man" is *ish*; "woman" is *ishah*. *Ishah* is not derived from *ish*, but it sounds like it. Biblical Hebrew was a poetic language. Its speakers and writers loved word plays, so it said that *ishah* was taken out of *ish*. Adam and Eve understood the implications of that.

2:24 leaves ... and bonds. From the beginning of creation, God established the order of the family. Just as Eve was made from Adam's own body, so when a couple is married the two become one. A man leaves his home, the roots from which he came, and establishes a new life with his new family. Even though polygamy was practiced in Old Testament times, it is clear from this verse that God's plan was for a man and a woman to become one in lifelong service and union.

PSALM 128:3-4

128:3 Your wife. Psalm 128 is called the marriage prayer because it was often sung at Jewish weddings. Marital bliss has always been one of the greatest blessings. *fruitful vine.* The main idea of this verse involves procreation, but the vine imagery relates to the garden themes common in the Song of Songs.

SONG OF SONGS 5:1C

Solomon spoke the first lines of this verse as he claimed the sexual favors of his wife. The final line contains the only words in the Song of Songs spoken directly by God as He heartily approved of their lovemaking.

1 CORINTHIANS 6:16-17

6:16 joined to. This verse suggests there is no such thing as casual sex. The man who thoughtlessly buys the services of a prostitute enters a serious, mysterious union with her. Accordingly, promiscuous behavior creates multiple unions that can never realize their intended meaning. *one body with her.* The physical union of sexual intercourse creates a physical bond. That physical bond should also represent an emotional and spiritual bond that cannot occur with a prostitute.

EPHESIANS 5:22-31
See next page

5:22 submit. This injunction from Paul must be understood in its historical context. In Jewish law, a woman was a "thing" not a person, and she had no legal rights. In Rome, too, divorce was easy and women were repressed. Against this, Paul proposed a radical, liberating view: (1) submission was to be mutual; (2) wives were called upon to defer only to their husbands (and not to every man); and (3) submission was defined by Christ's headship of the church (Christ died for the church). *to your own husbands.* A woman owes submission only to her husband, not to all men (as first-century culture taught).

5:23 Christ is head of the church. This is a headship of love, not of control; of nurture, not of suppression.

5:25 love your wives. This is the main thing Paul said to husbands. It is so important that he repeated this injunction three times (vv. 25, 28, 33). Paul urged a certain type of love: agape, which is characterized by sacrificial, self-giving action. *just as also Christ loved the church and gave Himself for her.* Two qualities characterized Christ's actions on behalf of the church: love and sacrifice. The husband is called upon to act toward his wife in the same way.

5:27 to present the church. At a Jewish wedding, the bride was presented to the groom by a friend.

5:28 their own bodies. Eve was Adam's flesh and bones—she came from his body. Believers in Christ are His body. When a man and a woman marry, they become "one flesh" (Genesis 2:24; Ephesians 5:31). The man's deep-rooted instinct to care for himself should carry over to her.

5:31 one flesh. Paul did not view marriage as some sort of spiritual covenant devoid of sexuality. His illustration of how a husband is to love his wife (vv. 28-31) revolved around their sexual union, as was made explicit here by his quotation of Genesis 2:24.

LEADER'S GUIDE

CONTENTS

WELCOME TO COMMUNITY!

Meeting together with a group of people to study God's Word and experience life together is an exciting adventure. A small group is ... *a group of people unwilling to settle for anything less than redemptive community.*

CORE VALUES

Community:
God is relational, so He created us to live in relationship with Him and each other. Authentic community involves *sharing life together* and *connecting* on many levels with the people in our group.

Group Process:
Developing authentic community requires a step-by-step process. It's a journey of sharing our stories with each other and learning together.

Stages of Development:
Every healthy group goes through various stages as it matures over a period of months or years. We begin with the *birth* of a new group, deepen our relationships in the *growth* and *development* stages, and ultimately *multiply* to form other new groups.

Interactive Bible Study:
God provided the Bible as an instruction manual of life. We need to deepen our understanding of God's Word. People learn and remember more as they wrestle with truth and learn from others. The process of Bible discovery and group interaction will enhance our growth.

Experiential Growth:

The goal of studying the Bible together is not merely a quest for knowledge; this should result in real life change. Beyond solely reading, studying, and dissecting the Bible, being a disciple of Christ involves reunifying knowledge with experience. We do this by bringing our questions to God, opening a dialogue with our hearts (instead of killing our desires), and utilizing other ways to listen to God speak to us (group interaction, nature, art, movies, circumstances, etc.). Experiential growth is always grounded in the Bible as God's primary means of revelation and our ultimate truth-source.

The Power of God:

Our processes and strategies will be ineffective unless we invite and embrace the presence and power of God. In order to experience community and growth, Jesus needs to be the centerpiece of our group experiences and the Holy Spirit must be at work.

Redemptive Community:

Healing best happens within the context of community and in relationship. A key aspect of our spiritual development is seeing ourselves through the eyes of others, sharing our stories, and ultimately being set free from the secrets and the lies we embrace that enslave our souls.

Mission:

God has invited us into a larger story with a great mission. It is a mission that involves setting captives free and healing the broken-hearted (Isaiah 61:1-2). However, we can only join in this mission to the degree that we've let Jesus bind up our wounds and set us free. As a group experiences true redemptive community, other people will be attracted to that group, and through that group to Jesus. We should be alert to inviting others while we maintain (and continue to fill) an "empty chair" in our meetings to remind us of others who need to encounter God and authentic Christian community.

STAGES OF GROUP LIFE

Each healthy small group will move through various stages as it matures. There is no prescribed time frame for moving through these stages because each group is unique.

Birth Stage: This is the time in which group members form relationships and begin to develop community.

Multiply Stage: The group begins the multiplication process. Members pray about their involvement in establishing new groups. The new groups begin the cycle again with the Birth Stage.

Growth Stage:
Here the group members begin to care for one another as they learn what it means to apply what they have discovered through Bible study, shared experiences, worship, and prayer.

Develop Stage: The Bible study and shared experiences deepen while the group members develop their gifts and skills. The group explores ways to invite neighbors, friends, and coworkers to meetings.

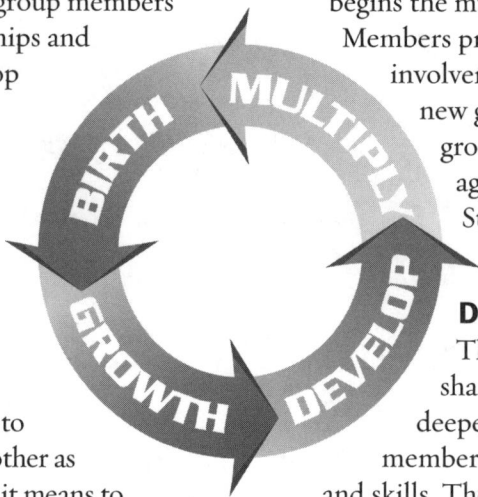

Subgrouping: If you have more than 12 people at a meeting, Serendipity House recommends dividing into smaller subgroups after the "Breaking the Ice" segment. Ask one person to be the leader of each subgroup, following the "Leader" directions for the session. The Group Leader should bring the subgroups back together for the closing. Subgrouping is also very useful when more openness and intimacy is required. The "Connecting" segment in each session is a great time to divide into smaller groups of four to six people.

SHARING YOUR STORIES

The sessions in *Dream Team* are designed to help you share a little of
your personal lives with the other people in your group
as you learn to build an amazing marriage. Through
your time together, each member of the group
is encouraged to move from low risk,
less personal sharing to higher risk
communication. Real community
will not develop apart from
increasing intimacy
of the group over
time.

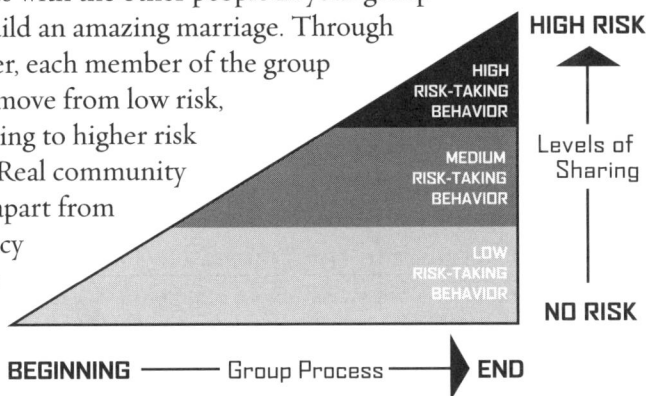

HIGH RISK

HIGH
RISK-TAKING
BEHAVIOR

Levels of
Sharing

MEDIUM
RISK-TAKING
BEHAVIOR

LOW
RISK-TAKING
BEHAVIOR

NO RISK

BEGINNING ——— Group Process ——➤ **END**

SHARING YOUR LIVES

As you share your lives together during this time, it is important to recognize
that it is God who has brought each person to this group, gifting the
individuals to play a vital role in the group (1 Corinthians 12:1). Each of you
was uniquely designed to contribute in your own unique way to building into
the lives of the other people in your group. As you get to know one another
better, consider the following four areas that will be unique for each person.
These areas will help you get a "grip" on how you can better support others
and how they can support you.

G – Spiritual Gifts: God has given you unique spiritual gifts (1 Corinthians
12; Romans 12:3-8; Ephesians 4:1-16; etc.).

R – Resources: You have resources that perhaps only you can share,
including skill, abilities, possessions, money, and time (Acts
2:44-47; Ecclesiastes 4:9-12, etc.).

I – Individual Experiences: You have past experiences, both good and
bad, that God can use to strengthen others (2
Corinthians 1:3-7; Romans 8:28, etc.).

P – Passions: There are things that excite and motivate you. God has given
you those desires and passions to use for His purposes (Psalm
37:4,23; Proverbs 3:5-6,13-18; etc.).

To better understand how a group should function and develop in these four
areas, consider going through the Serendipity study entitled *Great Beginnings*.

GROUP MEETING

Each of your group meetings will include a four-part agenda.

1. Breaking the Ice: This section includes fun, uplifting questions to warm up the group and help group members get to know one another better as they begin the journey of becoming a connected community. These questions prepare the group for meaningful discussion throughout the session.

2. Discovering the Truth: The heart of each session is the interactive Bible study time. The goal is for the group to discover biblical truths through open, discovery questions that lead to further investigation. The emphasis in this section is on understanding what the Bible says through interaction within your group.

To help the group experience a greater sense of community, it is important for everybody to participate in the "Discovering the Truth" and "Embracing the Truth" discussions. Even though people in a group have differing levels of biblical knowledge, it is vital that group members encourage each other share what they are observing, thinking, and feeling about the Bible passages. Scripture notes are provided at the end of each session to provide additional Bible understanding.

3. Embracing the Truth: All study should direct group members to action and life change. This section continues the Bible study time but with an emphasis on leading the group members toward integrating the truths they have discovered into their lives. The questions are very practical and application-focused.

4. Connecting: One of the key goals of this study is to lead group members to grow closer to one another as the group develops a sense of community. This section focuses on further application, as well as opportunities for encouraging, supporting, and praying for one another.

BONUS – Taking it Home:
Between each session, there is some homework for group members. This simply includes either a question to take to God or a question to take to your heart, as well as a date night for each couple. These experiences are designed to reinforce the content of the session and help couples strengthen their marriages.

Meeting Planner

The leader or facilitator of our group is _____ .
The apprentice facilitator for this group is _____ .

We will meet on the following dates and times:

	Date	Day	Time
Session 1	_____	_____	_____
Session 2	_____	_____	_____
Session 3	_____	_____	_____
Session 4	_____	_____	_____
Session 5	_____	_____	_____
Session 6	_____	_____	_____

We will meet at:

Session 1 _____
Session 2 _____
Session 3 _____
Session 4 _____
Session 5 _____
Session 6 _____

Childcare will be arranged by:

Session 1 _____
Session 2 _____
Session 3 _____
Session 4 _____
Session 5 _____
Session 6 _____

Refreshments will be arranged by:

Session 1 _____
Session 2 _____
Session 3 _____
Session 4 _____
Session 5 _____
Session 6 _____

GROUP COVENANT

As you begin this study, it is important that your group covenant together, agreeing to live out important group values. Once these values are agreed upon, your group will be on its way to experiencing true Christian community. It's very important that your group discuss these values—preferably as you begin this study. The first session would be most appropriate.

* **Priority:** While we are in this group, we will give the group meetings priority.

* **Participation:** Everyone is encouraged to participate and no one dominates.

* **Respect:** Everyone is given the right to his or her own opinions, and all questions are encouraged and respected.

* **Confidentiality:** Anything that is said in our meetings is never repeated outside the meeting without permission.

* **Life Change:** We will regularly assess our progress toward applying the "steps" to an amazing marriage. We will complete the "Taking it Home" activities to reinforce what we are learning and better integrate those lessons into our marriages.

* **Care and Support:** Permission is given to call upon each other at any time, especially in times of crisis. The group will provide care for every member.

* **Accountability:** We agree to let the members of our group hold us accountable to commitments we make in whatever loving ways we decide upon. Unsolicited advice giving is not permitted.

* **Empty Chair:** Our group will work together to fill the empty chair with an unchurched person or couple.

* **Mission:** We agree as a group to reach out and invite others to join us and to work toward multiplication of our group to form new groups.

* **Ministry:** We will encourage one another to volunteer to serve in a ministry and to support missions work by giving financially and/or personally serving.

I agree to all of the above＿＿＿＿＿＿＿＿＿＿＿＿＿＿ date: ＿＿＿＿＿＿

LEADER'S GUIDE

This section contains leader ideas, tips, and answers for "Discovering the Truth" and "Embracing the Truth" questions in each of the six sessions.

General Tips:

1. *Prepare* for each meeting by reviewing the material, praying for each group member, asking the Holy Spirit to join you at each meeting, and making Jesus the centerpiece of every experience.
2. *Connect* with group members away from group time. The amount of participation you have during your meetings is directly related to the amount of time you connect with people outside the meetings.
3. *Don't get impatient* about the depth of relationship group members are experiencing. Building real Christian Community takes time.
4. Should difficult *marital issues* surface, be prepared with names of pastors and Christian marriage counselors to whom you can refer couples.
5. Try to keep discussions from *getting bogged down*, but give priority to addressing any needs within your group through "spontaneous prayer" and group support. NOTE: You can ask whether your group would prefer to shorten an important discussion or extend the duration of your study.
6. *A great group leader* talks less than 10% of the time. If no one answers a question, just wait. If you create an environment where you fill the gaps of silence, the group will learn they needn't join you in the conversation.

Session 1: Generating "Heat"

DISCOVERING THE TRUTH:

1. This question helps group members recall the passion of newlyweds who want nothing more than expressing feelings and delighting in one another.

2. This question should elicit remarks about the importance of words, especially romantic words, for creating passionate feelings in women. Solomon's words also affirmed the high esteem in which he held his bride.

3. "Beauty is in the eye of the beholder" applies. We all are less than perfect physical specimens. We should praise our spouse for the delights he or she gives and the unique beauty or handsomeness we find in him or her.

4. In general, women are less compartmentalized than men. They view sex within the totality of the relationship. Genuine romance with tender words and tender touch help a wife understand how much she is valued.

5. As we become accustomed to one another, the sense of wonder that our spouse loves us can fade into the landscape of daily routine. We take the other's love for granted. As this happens, romantic feelings and passionate lovemaking are often replaced by obligatory sexual routines.

6. Good retreat locations can be private and breathtakingly beautiful, which inspires romantic feelings and heightens the enjoyment of a honeymoon. Note Solomon's invitation to his bride of safety and security in his arms.

7. Encourage group members to consider how to incorporate some of the concepts of the Song of Songs into their own romantic activities.

8. The real key to continuing to capture each other's hearts is intentionality and attentiveness to ongoing romance as vital to the health of a marriage.

EMBRACING THE TRUTH:

1. A locked garden is private and protected, so we expect it to be well-tended and lush. We expect a public garden to be worn from use. A sealed spring suggests clean, pure water. Solomon used both images to express his anticipation of his virgin bride. The garden is only unlocked to our spouse.

2. Her forthrightness may have resulted from how much she and Solomon had talked of their love during their engagement. She must have been secure in her sense of self, in Solomon's high regard for her, and in God's blessing on their union. Perhaps she had been well-coached in sexual arts by her mother.

3. Invite group members opinions. Communication is vital for understanding each other's needs and desires. Consideration is necessary if sexual love is to be an act of giving vs. an act of taking. Interestingly, the more we give to our spouse sexually, the more we will desire him or her.

Session 2: Striking the Match

DISCOVERING THE TRUTH:

1. Adam recognized in Eve what he could never find in any of the creatures he observed and named (Genesis 2:19-20). He found in her the rest of himself. That was literally true physically. It was more true emotionally and spiritually.

2. Eve was bone of Adam's bone and flesh of his flesh, so husbands and wives are to become one flesh. God intends male and female to complement one another in marriage. The Books of Proverbs and Ecclesiastes advise taking pleasure in one's spouse. Those whom God has designed for marriage find their greatest personal satisfaction in relationship with their mates.

3. Some see male initiative and female receptivity in sexual organs Some think reproduction is the greatest result of our union, so sex is a logical symbol of unity. Others say intimate, sexual contact requires generosity and kindness, as well as passion. This requires the best of masculine and feminine qualities.

4. We're amazingly complex and we change all the time. When we become students of our spouses, we learn new and deeper things about them as long as we live. If intimacy grows out of love that focuses on and understands the beloved, it can grow and deepen through a lifetime.

5. Life "under the sun" is the daily grind of struggle and disappointment in a fallen world. Knowing our spouses understand, appreciate, and cherish us despite all circumstances brings a measure of grace and peace to our lives.

6. God wants the best for us. Proverbs 5:15-17 highlights the folly of sexual immorality. Sex outside of marriage misuses and abuses what God intended for us. Jesus and Paul look more at the spiritual aspects of immorality—how it defiles the Holy Spirit's home, giving Satan access and exposes us to judgment.

7. This question invites thinking about a concept we too quickly assume we understand. If people choose the same answer, you won't have much discussion. But if people look at it differently, it could be enlightening.

8. Ask your group to pool biblical knowledge about sexual attitudes and actions that harm marriage: adultery, flirtation, sexual fantasies, porn, etc.

EMBRACING THE TRUTH:
1. Peter expected wives to know the condition of their husbands' hearts; to be persuasive examples vs. pushy; to lead pure and reverent lives. Key discussion: how to gain this knowledge from personal observation, time with God, family, mentoring women, small groups, church, Christian media, etc.

2. Women accept a vulnerable position when they submit to their husbands. Peter expected husbands to understand their wives' strengths and weaknesses as loving leaders. He is responsible for spiritually building, protecting, and honoring his wife. If he refuses, the Lord is not inclined to hear his prayers.

3. Pay attention to the issues raised here and how people react to them. You may want to encourage some to think further about matters that seem to touch them significantly.

4. This asks people to share ways they have found effective in gaining insight into their spouses. Hopefully, everyone will pick up a new idea or two.

Session 3: A Combustible Mixture

DISCOVERING THE TRUTH:
1. Stimulate a man visually and "ding" he's aroused. Arousal for women is a generally more complex process that builds over time. From a wife's view, sex is typically not an event to be rushed into or hurried through.

2. Questions 2-5 probe differences between men and women. Be careful that this doesn't become a bashing session. This question might elicit responses about harsh and dictatorial leadership, which crushes a wife's spirit, or leadership that never consults and so devalues a wife's opinions.

3. This question invites group members to observe how they perceive men and women to approach relationships differently.

4. Both husbands and wives can become bitter against one another. Male bitterness can be more aggressive and dangerous. God expects husbands to lead and take the responsibility of preventing such harshness and bitterness.

5. Husbands and wives are different by design to complement and complete each other. These differences are intended to deepen the relationship and draw us into maturity as we open up with one another.

6. Delilah most likely had learned Samson had too little self-control and too much self-confidence. She also probably figured if she persisted he would eventually give in, assuming he could muscle his way out of any problem.

7. All of the responses to this multiple-choice question are possible. Perhaps they all operate to some extent. Discussing the options should deepen group insight into Samson's weak character.

8. Samson and Delilah responded to non-verbal communications as well as verbal ones. So do all married couples. Husbands and wives should be alert to "signals." Intentionally ignoring signals can be a way of giving the cold shoulder or showing who is in control, causing frustration or hurt.

9. Samson used variations on "if-you-confine-me-like-this-I-become-weak-as-an-ordinary-man." Men tend to look for repeatable patterns and combinations. Women want personal connection and a husband's attentiveness.

EMBRACING THE TRUTH:
1. Solomon used tender words to let his bride know he was reading her signals. He clearly conveyed how enamored and excited he was with her.

2. Solomon's bride used words as well to express her offer of herself to her husband ... probably accompanied with the corresponding body language.

3. This question should generate further understanding about differences between men and women as well as differences between individuals. Be the first to share on (a very general level) to set the tone for the discussion.

Session 4: Stoking the Flames

DISCOVERING THE TRUTH:
1. Sex is typically a gauge that shows the condition of a marriage relationship. To help people ask this: "What can happen if we don't meet each other's needs?"

2. Answers will vary. Problems occur in one of two directions: demanding something sexually that one's spouse doesn't want to do or refusing something sexually that shouldn't be refused. *Session 5 focuses on this.*

3. If a husband has authority over his wife's body and she over his, they must agree on all that occurs between them. Better communication equals better sexual agreement. The poorer their communication, the more chances for

misunderstanding and frustration. Treating each other with honor and courtesy will enhance understanding and sexual harmony.

4. Answers will vary. Satan wants us to doubt the love of our spouse. He uses fear, frustration, anger, malice, and every evil attitude to weaken and destroy marriages. When sexual activity ceases for a long period at least one partner feels neglected.

5. Each should be available to satisfy romantic and sexual needs for the other. Availability doesn't mean marriage partners are sexual vending machines. It refers to glad willingness to respond to appropriate overtures. Distance is communicated through lack of communication, preoccupation, keeping to yourself, ignoring signals, insensitivity, dutiful vs. willing response, etc.

6. When one is inconsiderate and demanding sexually, it means selfish, unloving attitudes are at work. Impatience, unkindness, accepting false truths, vengeance, finding pleasure in evil, etc. may fuel sexual selfishness.

7. One can quietly hope bad things for one's spouse, keep a record of wrongs, and manipulate situations to get one's way.

8. This question asks group members to make a choice and explain it. Be aware of gender differences in the responses if there are any.

9. Consideration ties back to availability. Love for a spouse puts the other's needs ahead of our own. That could mean constraining yourself or giving of yourself as you look to the current needs of your husband or wife.

EMBRACING THE TRUTH:
1. She felt confident Solomon would return because she was his garden of delights. Their commitment and passion would pave the way to resolution.

2. He was glad that they belonged to each other. He was in awe of his bride's loveliness and the love and depth in her eyes. He didn't want to be separated from her because of personal pride over who won an argument.

3. He was daring in his use of romantic words in sharing his heart. She was daring in the way she abandoned herself to him.

Session 5: Fire Safety

DISCOVERING THE TRUTH:
1. Boundaries become much more important to us ours are violated.

2. Note that Jesus always invites: He knocks; He offers and waits to be received; He offers and then He always honors our boundaries and freedom to choose.

3. We're responsible to help others and work for their good, but we are each responsible for carrying our own loads. Without boundaries irresponsibility can thrive, but we all have excess burdens that require other's help.

4. Like a good wine, marriage handled the way God intends gets better and more precious with age. Picture "being lost in her love forever" – there's a depth of relationship that only comes with time, commitment, and desire.

5. Ruined reputations, unwanted pregnancies, STDs, God's judgment, etc. The most serious consequence is the deep soul-level damage that happens to each person in the picture. God wants us to avoid this hurt to ourselves and others.

6. Examples: Build into your marriage; No time alone with the opposite sex; Boundaries for touch; Discuss temptations early with your spouse and pray for each other; Accountability partners; Avoid emotional affairs; Guard the media channels to your eyes and heart; Run from temptation.

EMBRACING THE TRUTH:

1. When marital partners exercise authority over each other's bodies in a spirit of Christlike love, they give consideration to each other's desires and sensitivities. Each will desire to please the other and respect boundaries.

2. God is all about redemption, love, and freedom. With God in the center of our relationship there should be freedom and grace. Fear and love can't coexist. Our bedrooms should be filled with God's love and freedom.

3. If one spouse demands without regard for the other's feelings, the offended spouse will lose respect. Sex in this case will not be characterized by romance and love, but by dutiful, impersonal performance.

4. Consistently refusals fill marriage with frustration. The refused mate may become bitter and susceptible to temptation (e.g. adultery, flirtation, sexual fantasy, or porn). Deprive each other only by mutual consent for a short time of focused prayer. Any "no" really needs to be a "no now, but later" response.

5. Responses will vary based upon individual experiences. Be sure to keep the discussion short and focused on general responses vs. personal.

6. The cure to selfishness is becoming more like Christ. Develop mutual goals instead of imposing your own. Submit to the Holy Spirit, putting your spouse's interests ahead of your own, and giving honor and esteem to him/her.

Session 6: A Cozy Bonfire

DISCOVERING THE TRUTH:

1. Adam must have expected emotional *and* spiritual unity. Eve came from him and corresponded to him in every way. He expected to feel joy as they gave and received perfect love and to delight in God every day with Eve.

2. "One flesh" refers to physical union, but goes deeper to oneness and intimacy at heart and soul levels. Divorce damages the whole *and* both parts. Two working as one make life more bearable and shares the load (Eccl. 4:9-12).

3. Genesis 2:24 is God's explanation of the meaning of Adam and Eve's union to all succeeding generations. Jesus and Paul used this to point to fundamental realities of God's creation, sanction, and purpose in marriage.

4. Sex is more than just a physical act, with intertwining connection to our minds, hearts, and souls. Sex outside of marriage makes deep impacts on our marriage relationship, our relationship with Jesus, and specifically in a way other sins don't ourselves at a deep soul-level. God extends grace and redeems us of past mistakes, but there are deep wounds and consequences.

5. Solomon was describing the sweetness of the pleasure he anticipated from being with his wife. He also implied that his love, if not his soul, would be nourished and strengthened by the physical relationship they enjoyed.

6. The "one flesh" union again points to the physical, but is more focused on commitment, love, teamwork, emotional support, and spiritual connection. Look carefully at providing and caring phrases in Ephesians 5:22-31.

7. This verse commands a change of allegiance in marriage from our family of origin to our "one flesh" relationship. Sexual union reflects a deep, personal connection. Sex requires vulnerability and intimacy, mirroring and also gauging the level of closeness and intimacy in the relationship as a whole.

8. Solomon's words suggest that a husband and wife find refuge in their physical relationship. Each knows someone unconditionally loves and accepts him or her. A loving sexual relationship reinforces a sense of security and peace.

EMBRACING THE TRUTH:

1. Possible answers: A complex, Trinitarian God created a complex, 2-gender humanity. A sovereign God made creatures to represent Him as rulers of His creation. Perhaps God saw in Adam and Eve the essential features of personality that reflected Him just as He wanted them to. Sexuality plays a key role in expressing essential unity within this diverse creation.

2. The "fruitful vine" easily pictures childbearing, because vines bear grapes. It portrays feminine sexuality in the same way as the garden imagery in Song of Songs. Vines are most beautiful and sensually attractive when loaded with luscious fruit. See 1 Kings 4:25, Micah 4:4, and Zechariah 3:10.

3. God's blessing on the family in Psalm 128 is much more than a marriage contract and numerous children. The husband and wife in this psalm take delight in one another, as well as in their children. Marriage intimacy is called "a blessing" and "your portion;" it's intended to be a joy in life.

4. God endorses the sexual passion and pleasure of this couple in the same sensual (and nourishing) language they have used in the course of their lovemaking. "Friends" refers to the readers of the Song too, so God recommends the same passion and pleasure for all husbands and wives.

About the Author

Since 1977, Tommy Nelson has been the Pastor of Denton Bible Church, located in Denton, Texas. He has been featured on "Focus on the Family," "FamilyLife Today," "Life Outreach," and other national broadcasts.

In addition to the teaching series on Song of Solomon and A Life Well Lived (on Ecclesiastes), he is the author of several books including: *The Book of Romance*, *The Big Picture*, *The Musings of an Evangelical Mind*, *The 12 Essentials of Godly Success*, and *A Life Well Lived*.

Tommy graduated from the University of North Texas with a Bachelor's Degree in Education. He attended Dallas Theological Seminary in Dallas, Texas, where he received the Master of Arts in Biblical Studies degree.

Tommy has been married to Teresa Nelson for more than 30 years. They have two sons, one grandson, and one granddaughter.

Acknowledgments

Tommy Nelson and Serendipity House Publishing wish to thank the team of writers, editors, and designers that labored together to create this resource. Joe Snider and Ben Colter worked with Tommy Nelson to translate this content into a small-group experience. Other key contributors on the editorial team were: Ron Keck, Cathy Tardif, and Jenna Anderson. Scott Lee provided art direction and interior design. David Carlson of Studio Gear Box developed the cover design.

CREDITS

Serendipity and Tommy Nelson made use of the following resources in developing the Home...Works Series:

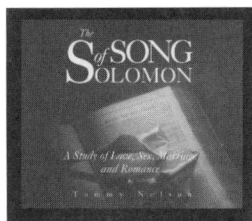

The Song of
 Solomon Series
 © 1995
 Hudson Productions

Maximum Marriage
 Series
 © 2004
 Tommy Nelson

Home...Works Series

In a world that competes for nearly every minute of our time and energy while offering so many choices on how to order our lives, it's sometimes hard to figure out what works. Our homes, kids, careers, and even church life all have the potential to take us out of balance if not managed according to God's Word and instruction. Why is this important to us? Why should it be important to you? Because God is radically in love with His family. And He is radically in love with your family.

And because home still works.

- ✠ *Some Assembly Required: Instructions for an Amazing Marriage*
- ✠ *Dream Team: The Power of Two*
- ✠ *Turning Up the Heat: Rekindle Romance and Passion*

GROUP DIRECTORY

Write your name on this page. Pass your books around and ask your group members to fill in their names and contact information in each other's books.

Your Name: _____

Name: _____
Address: _____
City: _____
Zip Code: _____
Home Phone: _____
Mobile Phone: _____
E-mail: _____

Name: _____
Address: _____
City: _____
Zip Code: _____
Home Phone: _____
Mobile Phone: _____
E-mail: _____

Name: _____
Address: _____
City: _____
Zip Code: _____
Home Phone: _____
Mobile Phone: _____
E-mail: _____

Name: _____
Address: _____
City: _____
Zip Code: _____
Home Phone: _____
Mobile Phone: _____
E-mail: _____

Name: _____
Address: _____
City: _____
Zip Code: _____
Home Phone: _____
Mobile Phone: _____
E-mail: _____

Name: _____
Address: _____
City: _____
Zip Code: _____
Home Phone: _____
Mobile Phone: _____
E-mail: _____

Name: _____
Address: _____
City: _____
Zip Code: _____
Home Phone: _____
Mobile Phone: _____
E-mail: _____

Name: _____
Address: _____
City: _____
Zip Code: _____
Home Phone: _____
Mobile Phone: _____
E-mail: _____

Name: _____
Address: _____
City: _____
Zip Code: _____
Home Phone: _____
Mobile Phone: _____
E-mail: _____

Name: _____
Address: _____
City: _____
Zip Code: _____
Home Phone: _____
Mobile Phone: _____
E-mail: _____

Name: _____
Address: _____
City: _____
Zip Code: _____
Home Phone: _____
Mobile Phone: _____
E-mail: _____

Name: _____
Address: _____
City: _____
Zip Code: _____
Home Phone: _____
Mobile Phone: _____
E-mail: _____